Autism & PDD™ Concept Development
Household Items

by Pam Britton Reese and Nena C. Challenner

Skills
- concept development
- language

Ages
- 3 through 8

Grades
- PreK through 3

Evidence-Based Practice

- Early intervention that addresses skill acquisition in the areas of interaction, attention, play, comprehension, and expression will support the development of an even profile. The acquisition of key developmental skills supports the later development of communication, language, and speech and enhances emotional, social, and academic development (RCSLT, 2005).

- Many children with autism spectrum disorders learn more readily through the visual modality (RCSLT, 2005).

- Students need to understand semantic connections among words for academic success (NRP, 2000).

- Vocabulary intervention should provide opportunities for students to use target words in multiple contexts (Boone et al., 2007).

Autism & PDD Concept Development: Household Items incorporates these principles and is also based on expert professional practice.

References

Boone, K., Letsky, S., Wallach, S., Young, J., Gingrass, K., & Daly, C. (2007, November 28). *Role of SLP: A method of inclusion.* Paper presented at the 2007 ASHA National Convention. Retrieved March 24, 2009 from http://convention.asha.org/2007/handouts/1137_1371Letsky_Sarah__107277_Nov28_2007_Time_071812AM.ppt

National Reading Panel (NRP). (2000). *Teaching children to read: An evidence-based assessment of the scientific research literature on reading and its implications for reading instruction—Reports of the subgroups.* Retrieved March 24, 2009 from www.nichd.nih.gov/publications/nrp/upload/report.pdf

Royal College of Speech & Language Therapists (RCSLT). (2005). *Clinical guidelines for speech and language therapists.* Retrieved March 24, 2009 from www.rcslt.org/resources/clinicalguidelines

LinguiSystems

LinguiSystems, Inc.
3100 4th Avenue
East Moline, IL 61244
800-776-4332

FAX: 800-577-4555
Email: service@linguisystems.com
Web: linguisystems.com

Copyright © 2001 LinguiSystems, Inc.

All of our products are copyrighted to protect the fine work of our authors. You may only copy the student materials as needed for your own use. Any other reproduction or distribution of the pages in this book is prohibited, including copying the entire book to use as another primary source or "master" copy.

Printed in the U.S.A.

ISBN 10: 0-7606-0390-1
ISBN 13: 978-0-7606-0390-1

About the Authors

Pam Britton Reese, M.A., CCC-SLP, owns a private practice, CommunicAid Plus, where she provides speech and language services to children and adults. She is also an educational consultant to public and private schools. Pam has over nine years experience in the schools as a speech-language pathologist and teacher of the hearing-impaired. She has worked with children with autism and PDD since 1995. *Autism & PDD: Concept Development* is her fourth publication with LinguiSystems.

Nena C. Challenner, M.Ed., is a Community-Based Instruction Teacher and Inclusion Specialist. She has been a teacher for over 15 years and has taught preschool through second grade. She has worked with children with autism and PDD since 1995. Nena is also a reading consultant at CommunicAid Plus. *Autism & PDD: Concept Development* is her third publication with LinguiSystems.

Dedication

For the children at CommunicAid Plus (CAP Kids!)

Edited by Lauri Whiskeyman
Illustrations by Margaret Warner
Page Layout by Christine Buysse and Denise Stone

Table of Contents

Introduction 5

    Chair 9

    Table 21

    Couch 33

    Sink 45

    Toilet 57

    Refrigerator 69

    Bed 81

    Lamp 93

    Telephone 105

    Television 117

Extension Activity 129

Suggested Literature 136

Picture Communication Symbols (PCS) © 1981-2000.
Reprinted with the permission of Mayer-Johnson, Inc., P.O. Box 1579,
Solana Beach, CA 92075-7579, 1-800-588-4548, *www.mayer-johnson.com*

after	page 72
big	page 29
close	page 72
dark	page 101
finished	pages 113, 125
little	page 29
part	page 76

Introduction

In our work with children with autism, we were often surprised at misconceptions our students had about the world. For example, when 9-year-old Katie was asked, "What would you do if you saw a house on fire?" she answered, "Roast marshmallows." She had only experienced fire in this way and was unable to perceive that fire might also be dangerous, that it burns, or that it can heat a home. Other children with autism whom we have known didn't recognize a sitting dog as a dog or a rocking chair as a chair. These are concepts that typically-developing children are able to process through observing or listening to information and instantly linking to other learned concepts. We know that children with autism must be taught such language skills as naming attributes, placing words in appropriate categories, and giving descriptions.

It is well documented that children with autism learn more easily when information is presented in a visual format. The picture is constant and the child can view it until the concept is learned, as opposed to the transient nature of speech. Most books published for young children, however, do not teach the concepts the child with autism needs to learn. Although the stories are often engaging and the artwork of museum quality, they too often confuse the child with autism. Foxes that drive? Animals that wear clothing and talk? Cars with eyes? Although amusing, they are not a realistic depiction of our world. Often, too, the art is very complex with many extraneous details. (A list of some books we found that did a good job of teaching concepts is included on page 136.)

Each book in *Autism & PDD: Concept Development* covers 10 concepts around a theme:

- Animals
- Clothing
- Food
- Household Items
- Toys and Entertainment
- Transportation

Specific attributes and features of each concept are illustrated with large pictures, simple sentences, and picture symbols. In addition, there are questions to check comprehension and activities to help the child apply this knowledge to other contexts. These books were developed for professionals who work with children with autism, ages 3 through 8. However, these books can also be used with children who have language delays or language disorders caused by disabilities such as Down syndrome. Parents and caregivers can also use these books.

How to Use this Book

This book contains concepts about 10 different household items. Each concept is illustrated in both a large-page and mini-page format for making books to read to the child. We suggest that the large-page format be copied. Place the pages in plastic page protectors. Sliding a thin piece of cardboard or card stock into the pocket between the pages will stiffen the pages and make

Introduction, *continued*

them easier for young children to turn. Put the pages into folders with brads or three-ring notebooks to create a book. You may want to put a copy of the the first page of each unit on the front of the folder or notebook. The mini-pages can be made into small books for the children to take home after they've heard the story at school.

You may want to use all of the concepts in the book at one time to introduce or extend a thematic unit or you can select a specific concept to focus on. For example, a child might know dog and cat, but have no idea what a rabbit is! Remember to go at the child's pace. A child might need many lessons on chairs, for example, before moving on to other concepts in the book.

Comprehension Questions

A variety of comprehension questions (e.g., *yes-no, wh-, how*) follow each concept. The questions can be used in different ways. Some children may only be able to answer the *yes-no* questions. Some children may do better with the *wh-* and *how* questions. You can ask the questions after each concept is taught or after each page. If a child has difficulty answering a question, go through the targeted concept again and help him or her find the answer. Cue the child by pointing to the picture and/or text as you ask the question again.

Generalization Pages

Each concept has a generalization exercise. This exercise is designed to check the child's comprehension of the concept as well as to extend understanding of the concept to different forms and views. Many of the children we work with understand only one form of a concept: "That is a cat. That cat is gray. Thus, all cats must be gray or they are not cats." As you can see, that is a false generalization. By presenting variations of the same concept such as size, color, and position, the child learns to expand his or her mental definition of the concept.

After you read about the targeted concept, make a copy of the generalization page for the child. Read the directions aloud and have the child complete the page. Then encourage the child to describe the circled concepts. Depending on the child's level, the responses could be as simple as labeling "shirt" or as elaborate as "The shirt has long sleeves." You can also use the pictures on this page to point out the differences between the circled concepts.

Extension Activity

This activity is designed to extend instruction for any of the concepts in the book. Directions are found on the activity pages.

Introduction, continued

Suggested Literature

We have included a list of children's literature to help extend and promote generalization of the concepts to other contexts. These books were carefully chosen because of their simple text and realistic pictures. It is important to provide as many opportunities as possible for the child with autism to see and hear the concept. We have found that repeated exposure to the concepts in *Autism & PDD: Concept Development*, followed by other books with different pictures and texts, aids the child with autism in generalizing the concept to different contexts.

Closing

Remember that the concepts covered in the book can be taught in classrooms as well as group or individual therapy sessions. We hope that the children you work with enjoy the books as much as our students and clients do.

Pam and Nena

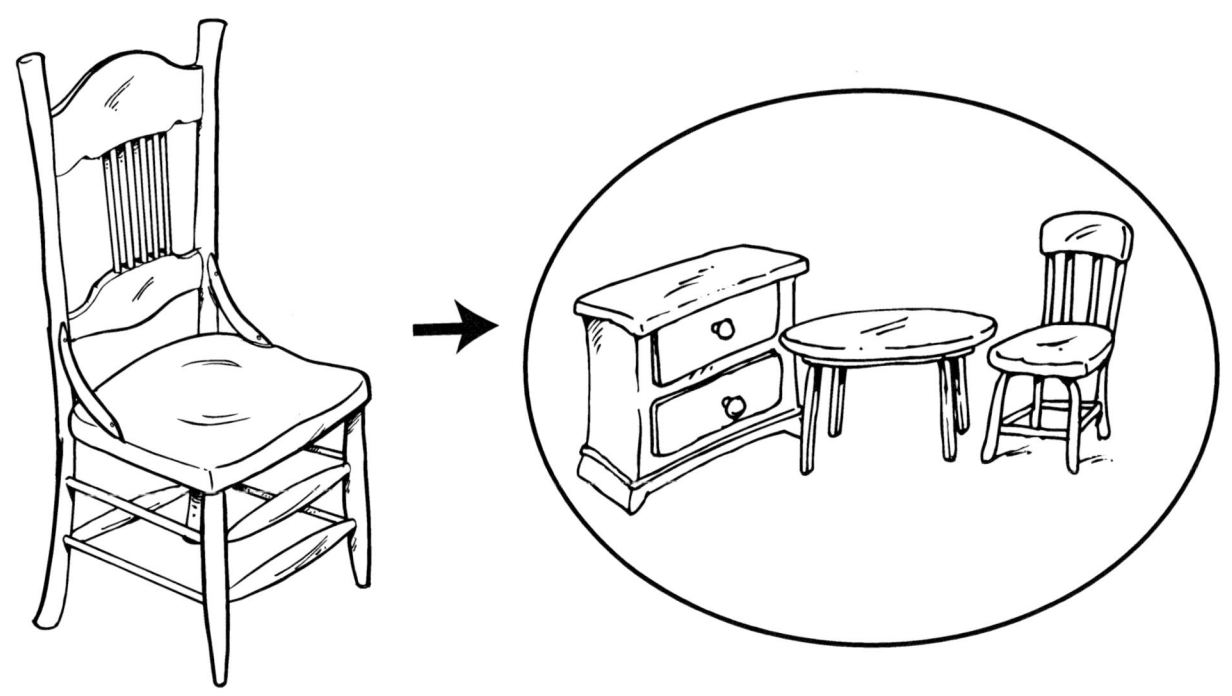

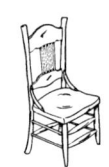 

A chair is a piece of furniture.

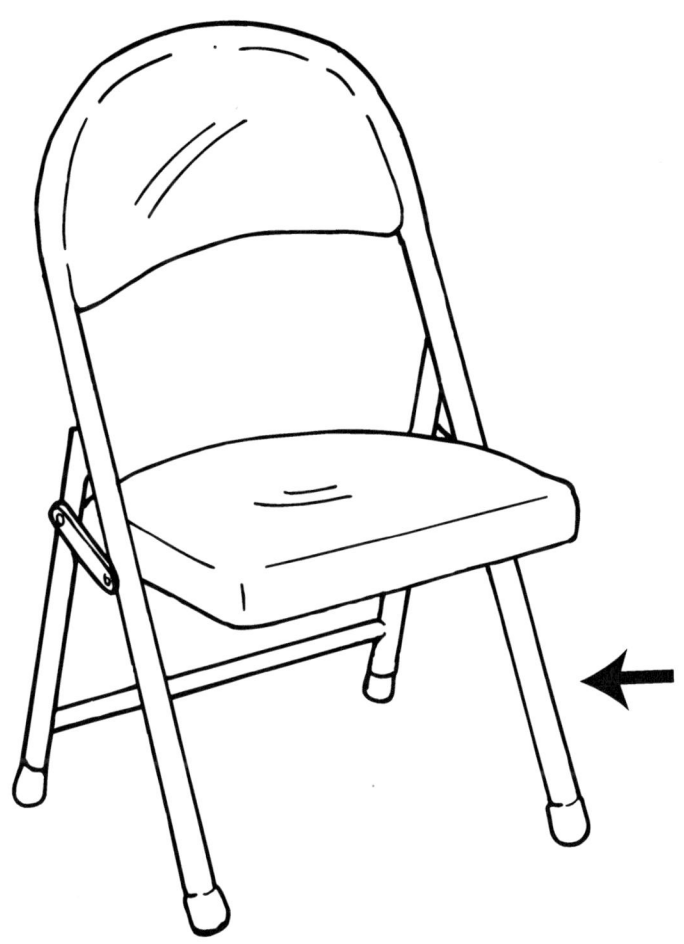

 4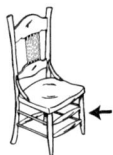

A chair has four legs.

 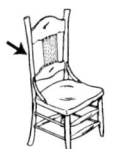 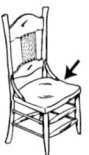

A chair has a back and a seat.

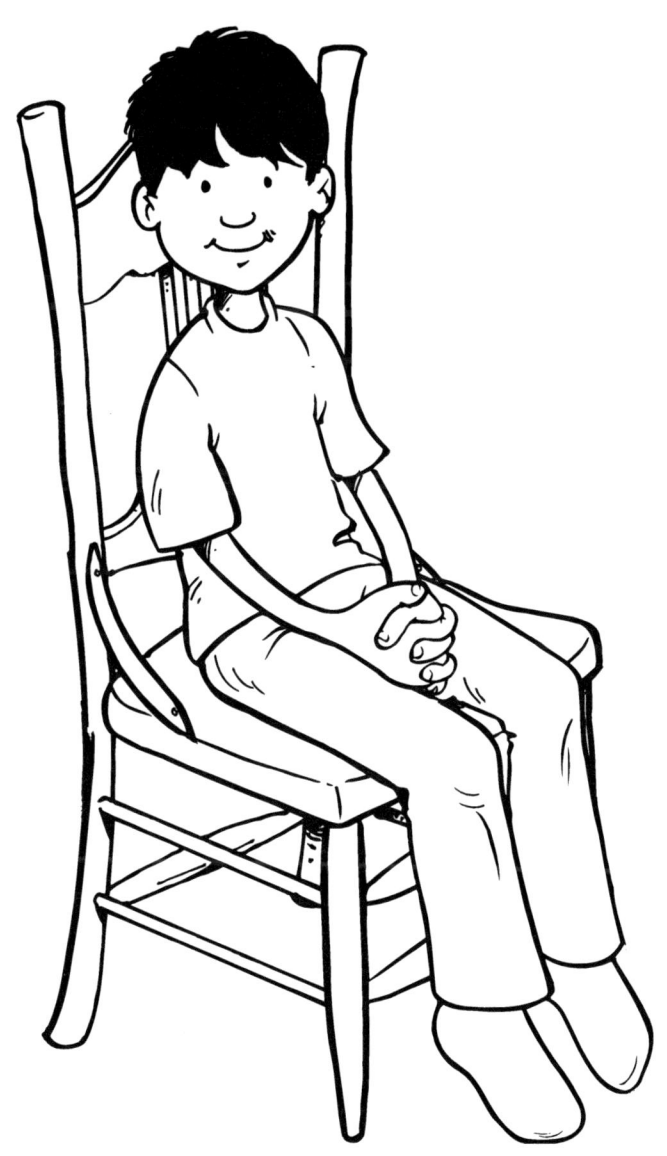

I sit on a chair.

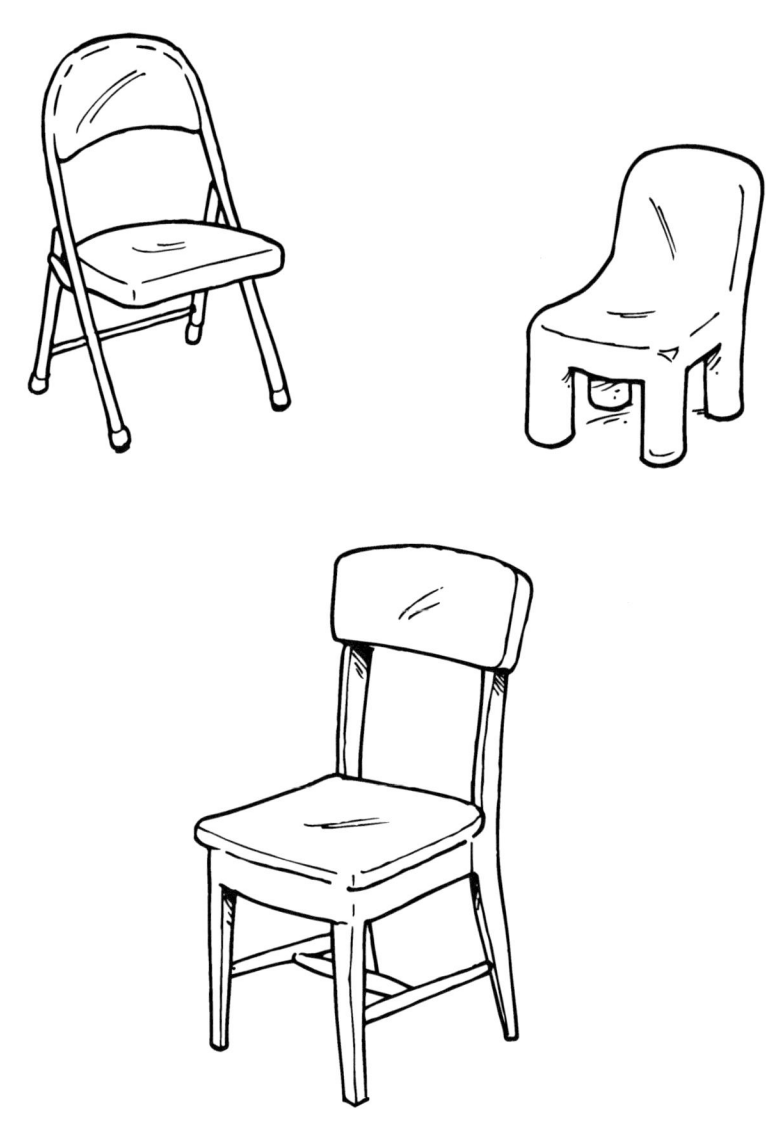

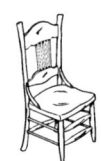   

Chairs are made of wood, metal, or plastic.

Sometimes chairs are soft too.

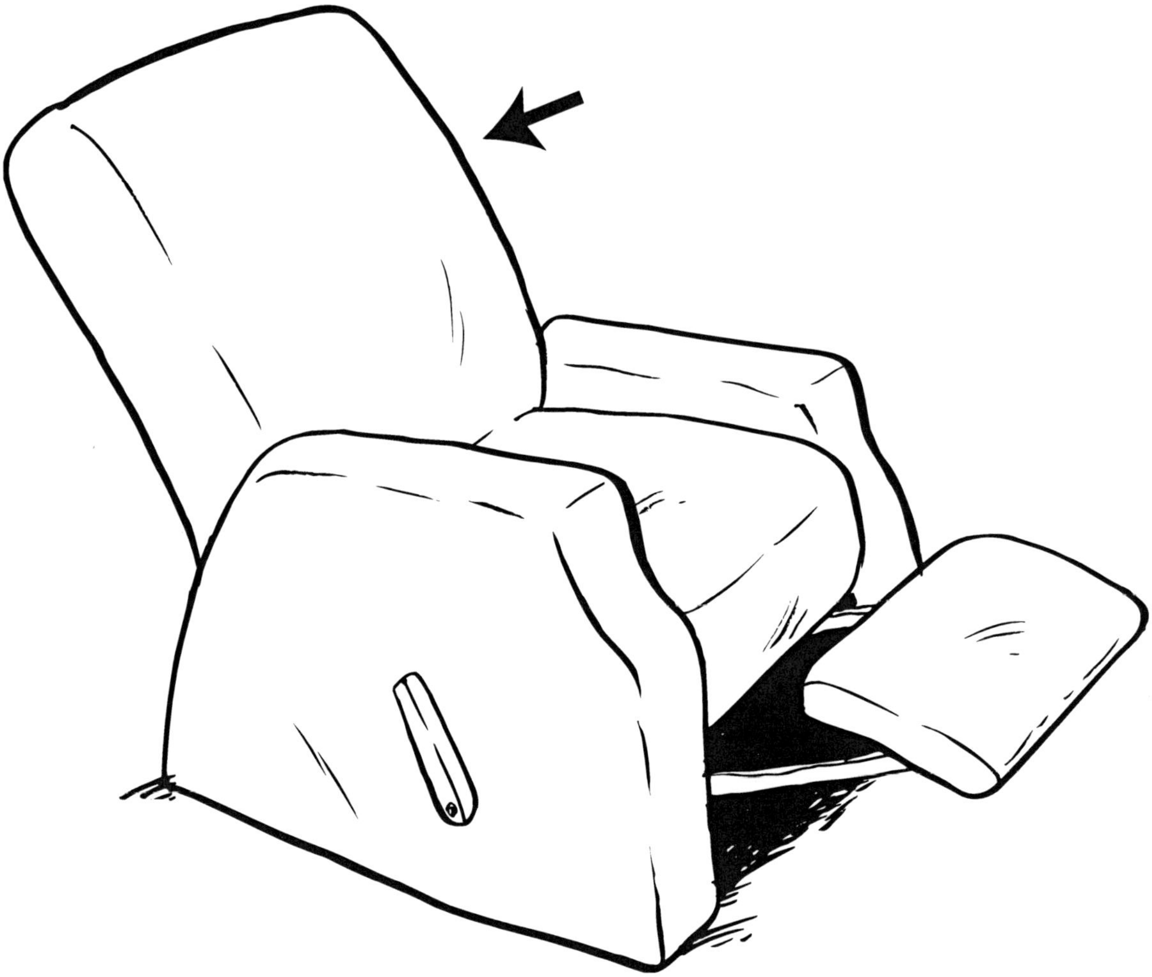

Some chairs recline.

Some chairs rock.

Concept: Chair

Yes-No Questions

1. Is a chair a toy?
2. Is a chair furniture?
3. Does a chair have two legs?
4. Does a chair have a back and a seat?
5. Do you sleep on a chair?
6. Are chairs made of wood?
7. Are chairs made of play dough?
8. Do some chairs rock?
9. Are some chairs soft?
10. Do you sit in chairs?

Wh- and How Questions

1. How many legs does a chair have?
2. What do you do with a chair?
3. What is a chair made of?
4. How do some chairs feel?
5. When does a chair rock?
6. What is a dog: clothing or an animal?
7. What does a chair have besides a back?
8. Where are chairs in a house?
9. Who sits on a chair?
10. Why do we have chairs?

Chair Generalization Page

Circle the chairs. Put an X on each picture that is not a chair.

Chair
Concept Development

Chair Mini-Book

Copy this page. Cut apart the boxes on the dotted lines. Put the story in order to make a little book and staple.

Chair

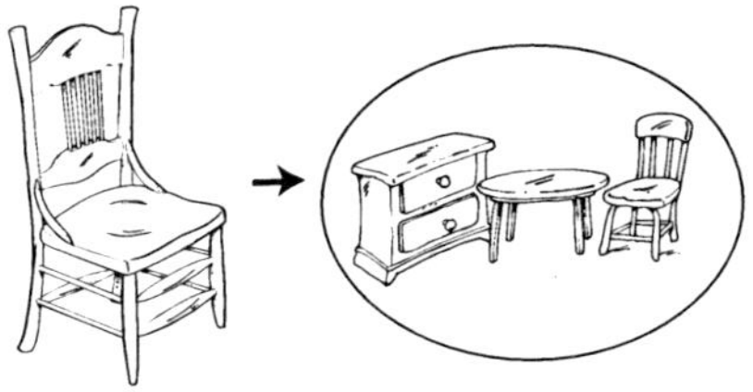

① A chair is a piece of furniture.

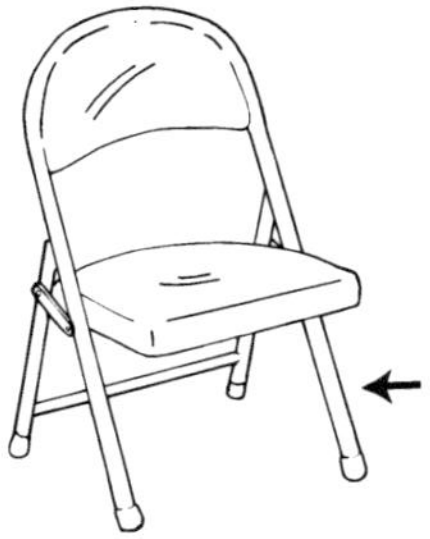

② A chair has four legs.

③ A chair has a back and a seat.

④ I sit on a chair.

⑤ Chairs are made of wood, metal, or plastic.

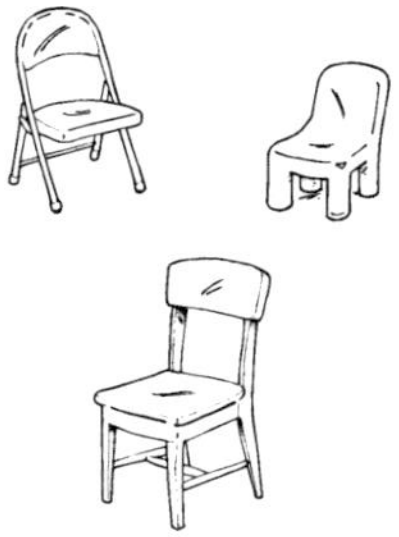

⑥ Sometimes chairs are soft too.

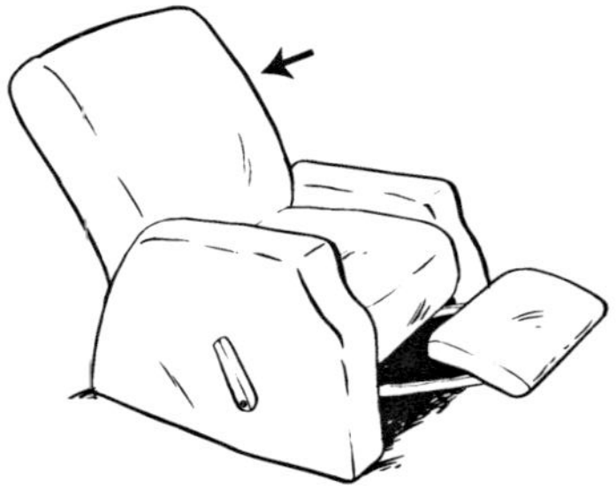

⑦ Some chairs recline.

⑧ Some chairs rock.

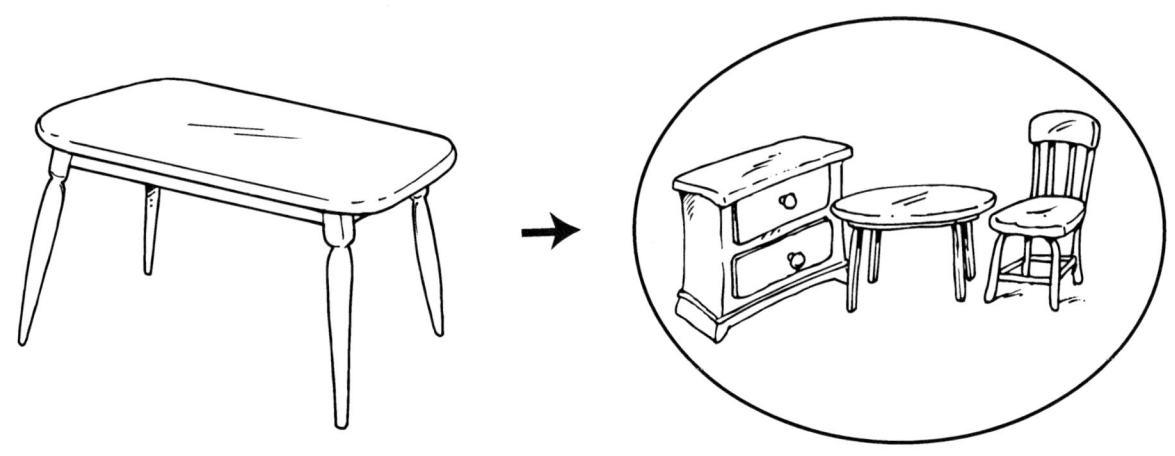

A table is a piece of furniture.

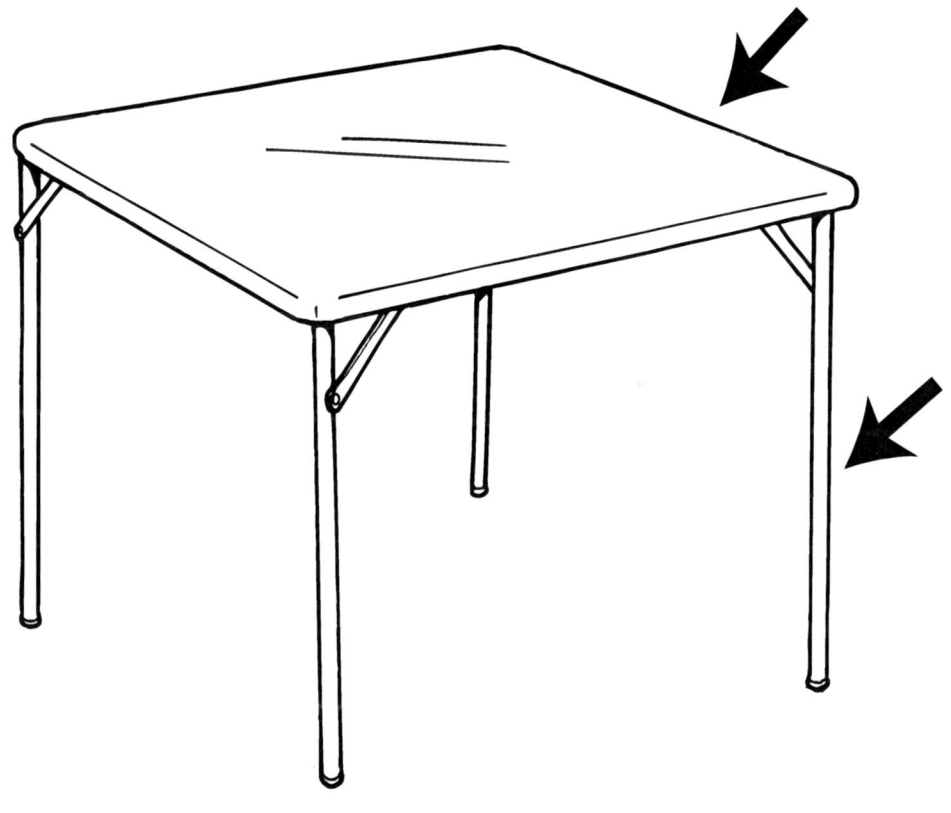

A table has four legs and a flat top.

Table

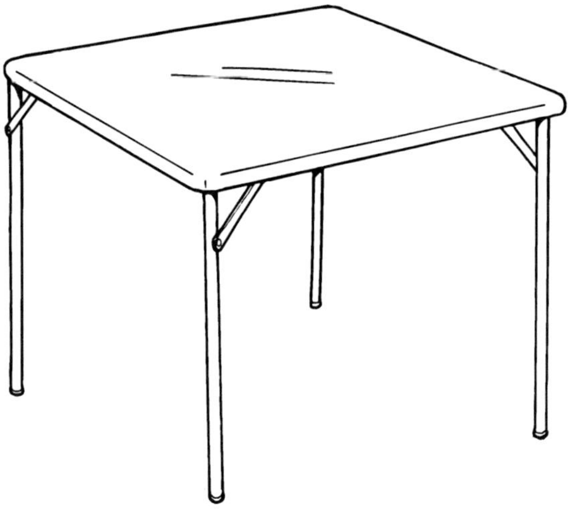

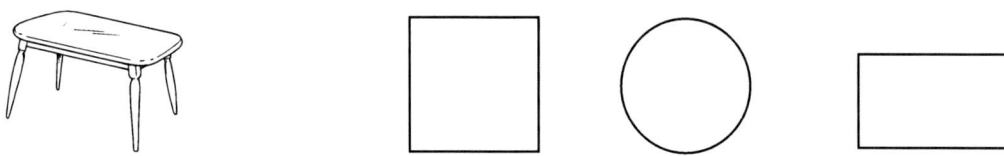

A table can be square, round, or rectangle.

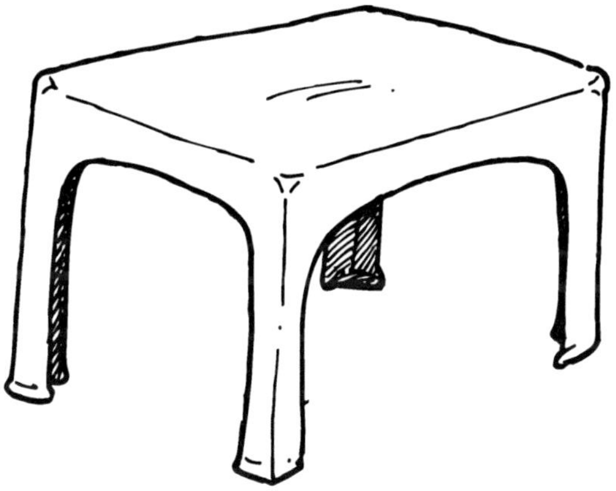

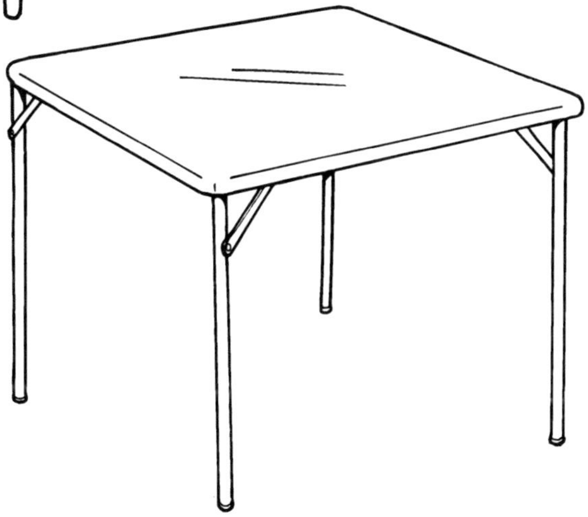

A table can be made of wood, metal, or plastic.

Table
Concept Development

I can sit in a chair to use a table.

I eat at a table.

Sometimes I work at a table.

 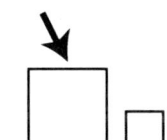 Some tables are big.  Some tables are little.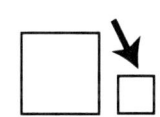

Concept: Table

Yes-No Questions

1. Is a table furniture?
2. Does a table have only three legs?
3. Does a table have a flat top?
4. Can a table be round?
5. Do we eat at a table?
6. Are some tables little?
7. Can a table be made out of plastic?
8. Do you sit in a chair at a table?
9. Do you sleep on a table?
10. Can you work on a table?

Wh- and How Questions

1. How many legs does a table have?
2. What kind of top does a table have?
3. Where is a table?
4. What is a table made of?
5. Where do we sit to use a table?
6. What can you do at a table?
7. Why do we have tables?
8. How are tables shaped: like squares or like triangles?
9. What shape is your table?
10. Who sits at a table?

Table Generalization Page

Circle the tables. Put an X on each picture that is not a table.

Table
Concept Development

Table Mini-Book

Copy this page. Cut apart the boxes on the dotted lines. Put the story in order to make a little book and staple.

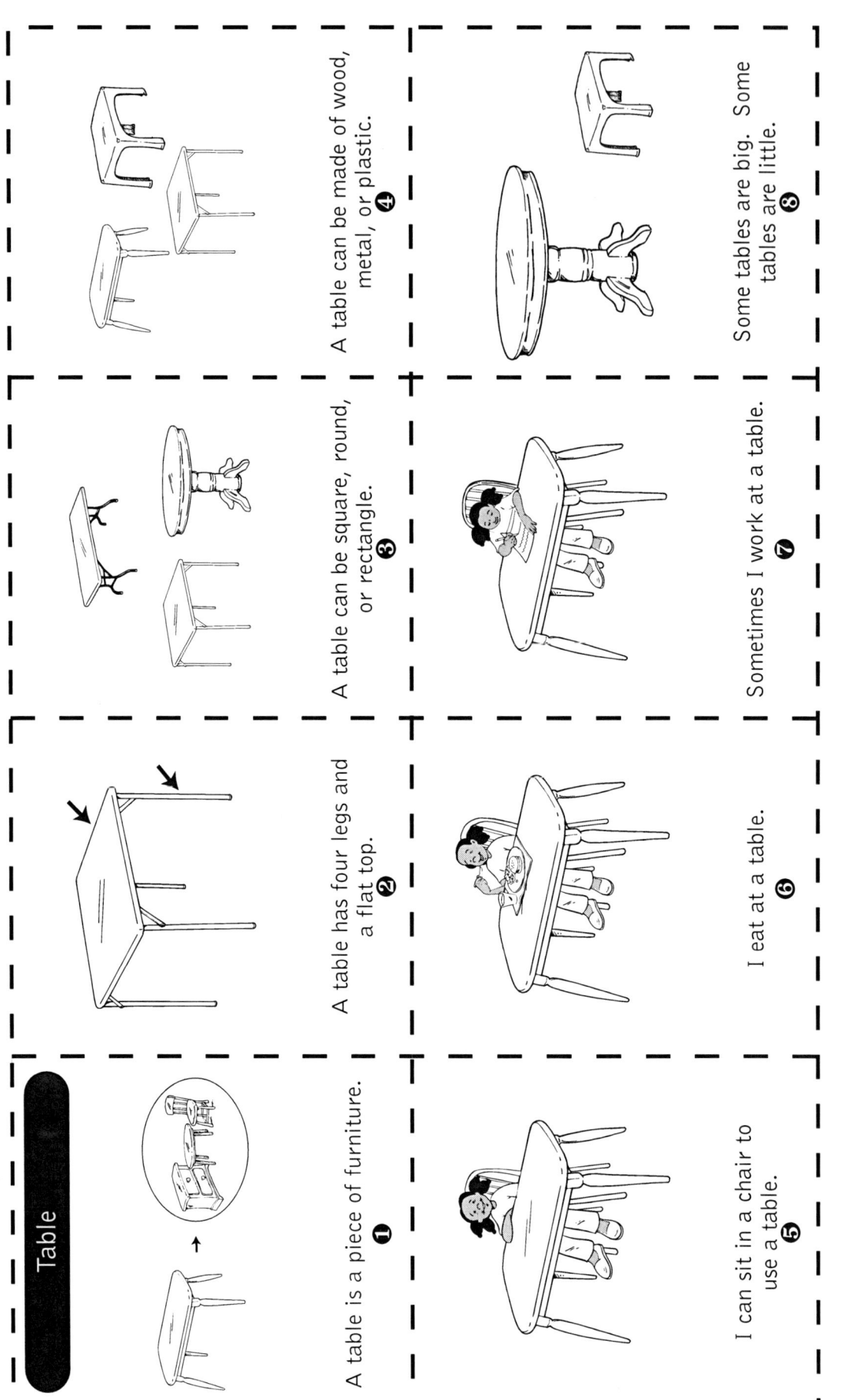

Table

① A table is a piece of furniture.

② A table has four legs and a flat top.

③ A table can be square, round, or rectangle.

④ A table can be made of wood, metal, or plastic.

⑤ I can sit in a chair to use a table.

⑥ I eat at a table.

⑦ Sometimes I work at a table.

⑧ Some tables are big. Some tables are little.

Table
Concept Development

Copyright © 2001 LinguiSystems, Inc.

Couch

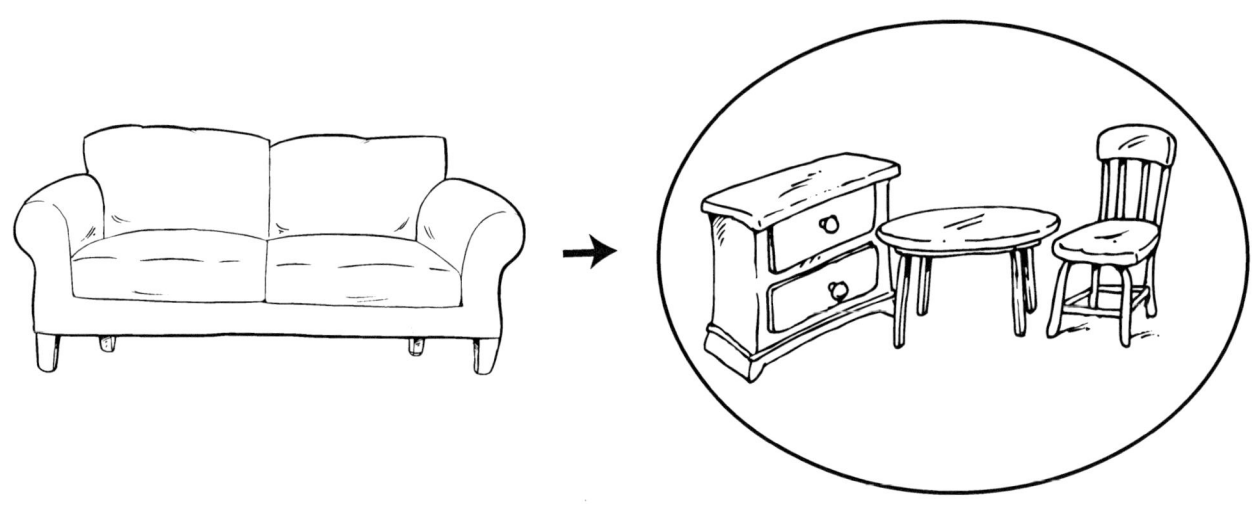

A couch is a piece of furniture.

 4

A couch has four legs.

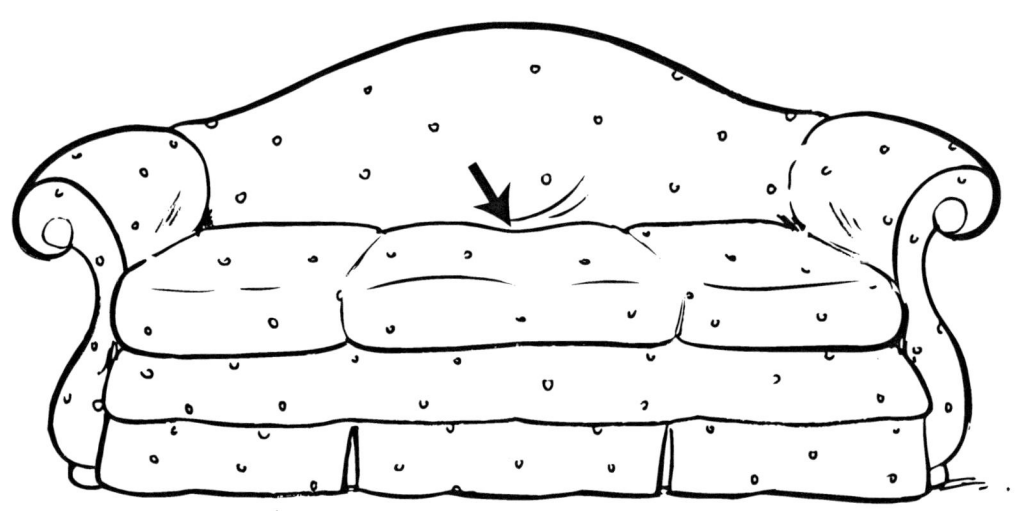

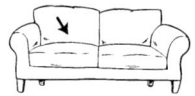

A couch has a long seat.

A couch has pillows.

A couch is in a living room.

I sit on a couch.

2 3

Two or three people can sit on a couch together.

  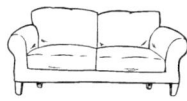

Sometimes people lie down on a couch.

Concept: Couch

Yes-No Questions

1. Is a couch clothing?
2. Is a couch a piece of furniture?
3. Does a couch have four legs?
4. Does a couch have cushions or pillows?
5. Do we dance on couches?
6. Is a couch in the bathroom?
7. Can two or three people sit on a couch?
8. Do you sit on a couch?
9. Do people sometimes lie down on a couch?
10. Does a couch have a long seat?

Wh- and How Questions

1. What is a couch?
2. How many legs does a couch have?
3. What kind of seat does a couch have?
4. Where is a couch?
5. How many people can sit on a couch?
6. What do you do with a couch?
7. Why do we have couches?
8. Where can people lie down?
9. What has pillows?
10. Who sits on a couch?

Couch Generalization Page

Circle the couches. Put an X on each picture that is not a couch.

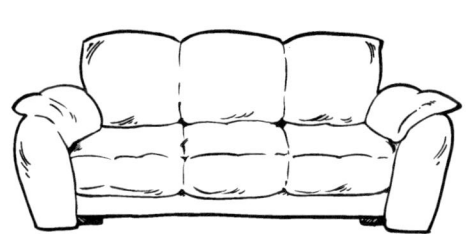

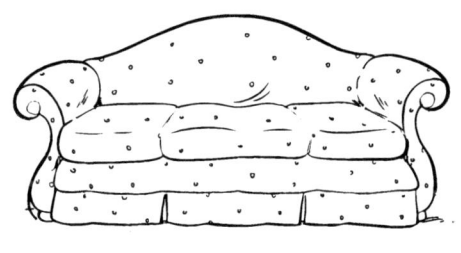

Couch Mini-Book

Copy this page. Cut apart the boxes on the dotted lines. Put the story in order to make a little book and staple.

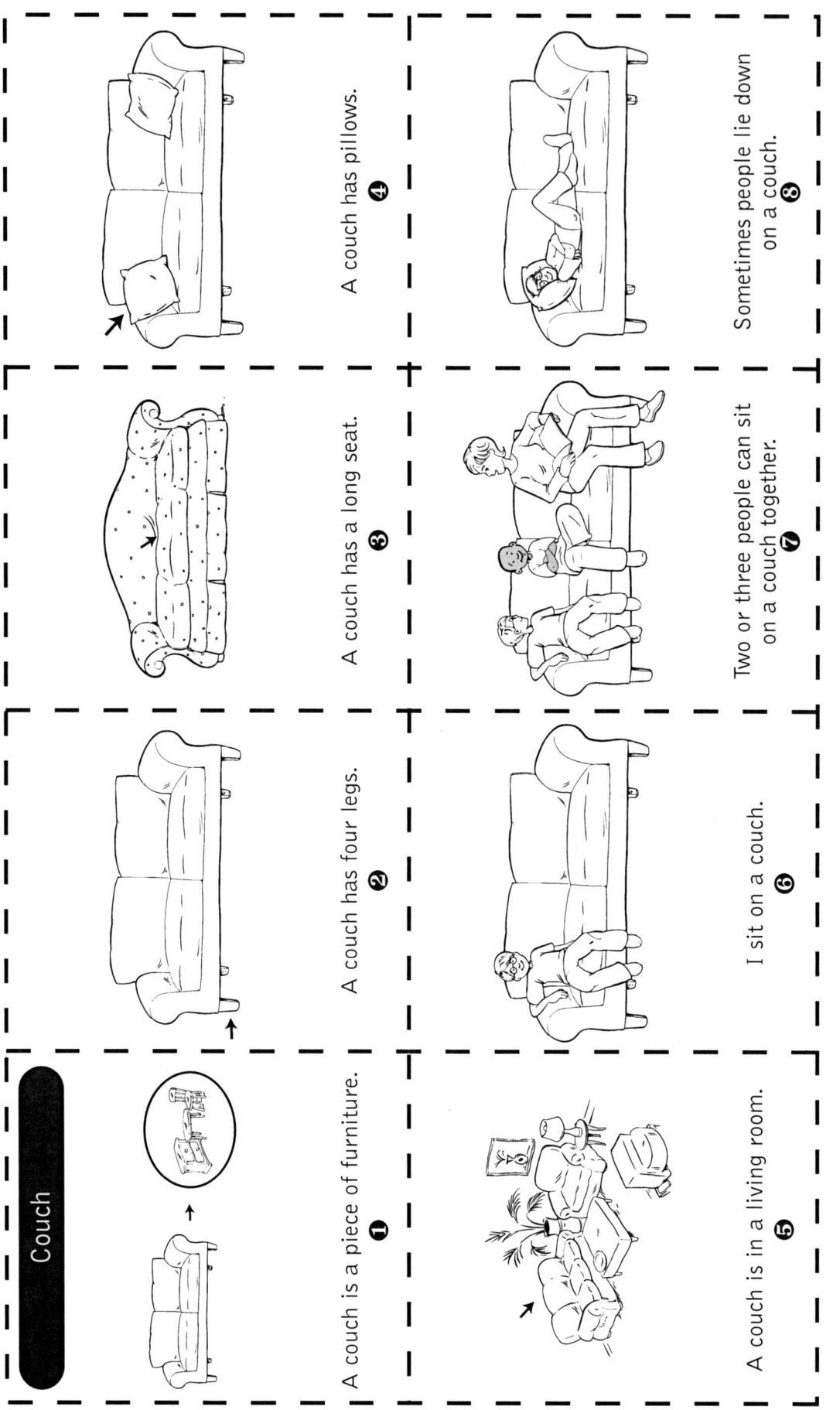

Couch

1. A couch is a piece of furniture.
2. A couch has four legs.
3. A couch has a long seat.
4. A couch has pillows.
5. A couch is in a living room.
6. I sit on a couch.
7. Two or three people can sit on a couch together.
8. Sometimes people lie down on a couch.

Copyright © 2001 LinguiSystems, Inc.

Couch
Concept Development

Sink

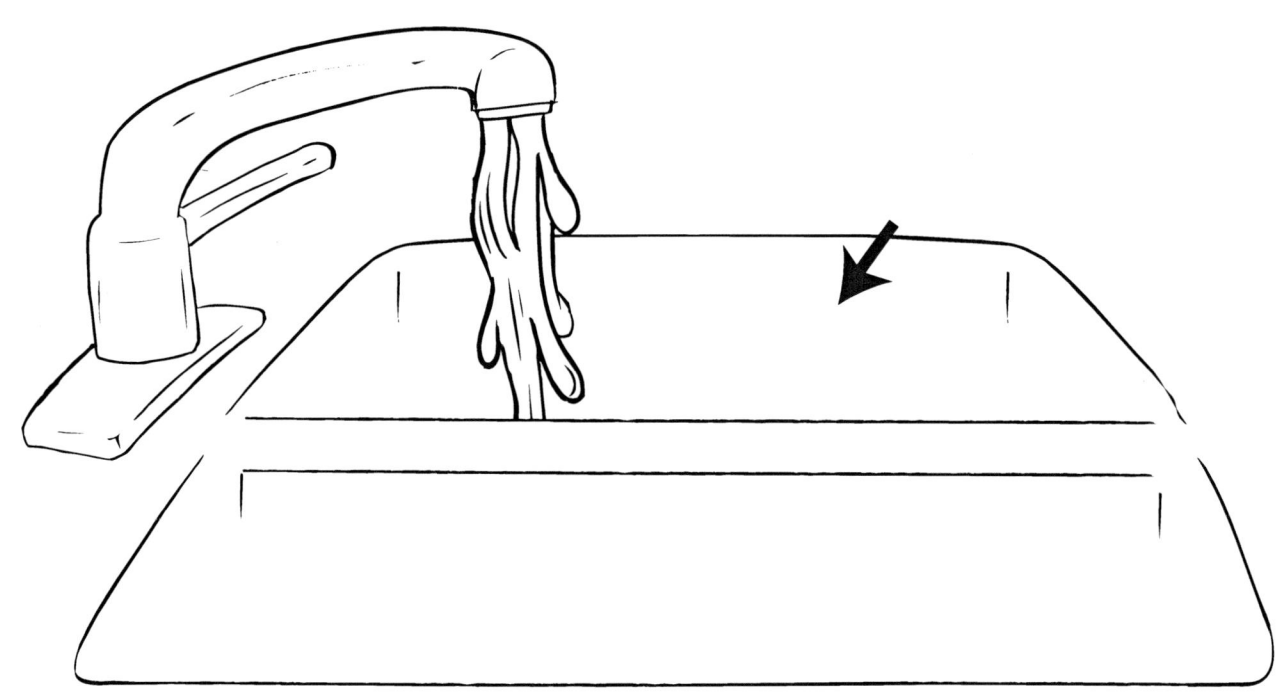

Water can come from a sink.

All of these are sinks.

Sink
Concept Development

A bathroom has a sink.

Sink

A kitchen has a sink.

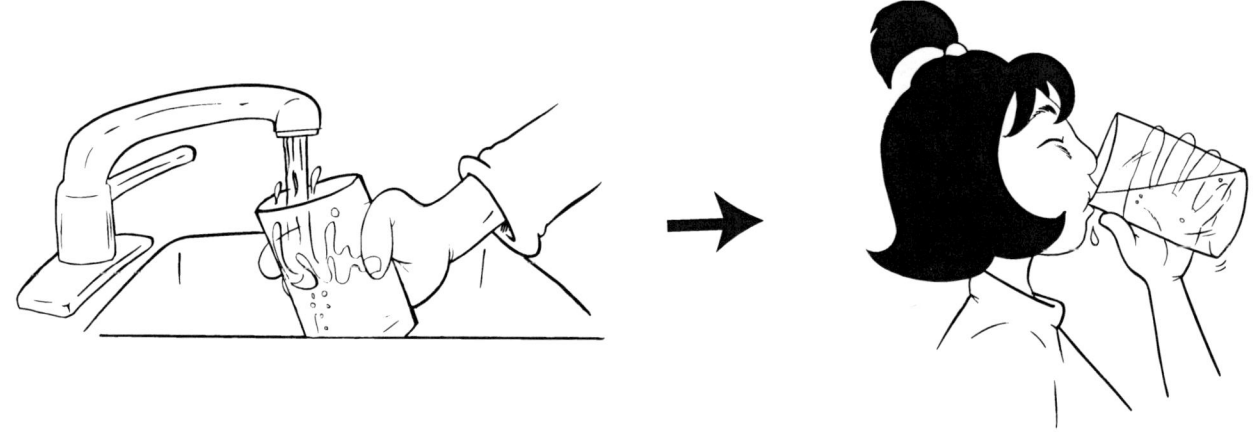

I drink water from a sink.

I can wash my hands in a sink.

I can wash dirty dishes in a sink.

I brush my teeth at a sink.

Concept: Sink

Yes-No Questions

1. Do you get cake from a sink?
2. Is a sink in a bathroom?
3. Is a sink in the bedroom?
4. Do you wash your hands in a sink?
5. Do you stand in a sink?
6. Do you brush your teeth at a sink?
7. Do you get water from a sink?
8. Do you wash cars in a sink?
9. Do you wash dirty hands in a sink?
10. Do you have a sink?

Wh- and How Questions

1. Where is a sink?
2. What comes from a sink?
3. Where do you wash your hands?
4. Where do you brush your teeth?
5. When do we wash dishes in the sink?
6. How do we wash dishes?
7. Who has a sink?
8. Why do we wash our hands?
9. Why do we brush our teeth?
10. Where can you get water?

Sink Generalization Page

Circle the sinks. Put an X on each picture that is not a sink.

Sink
Concept Development

Sink Mini-Book

Copy this page. Cut apart the boxes on the dotted lines. Put the story in order to make a little book and staple.

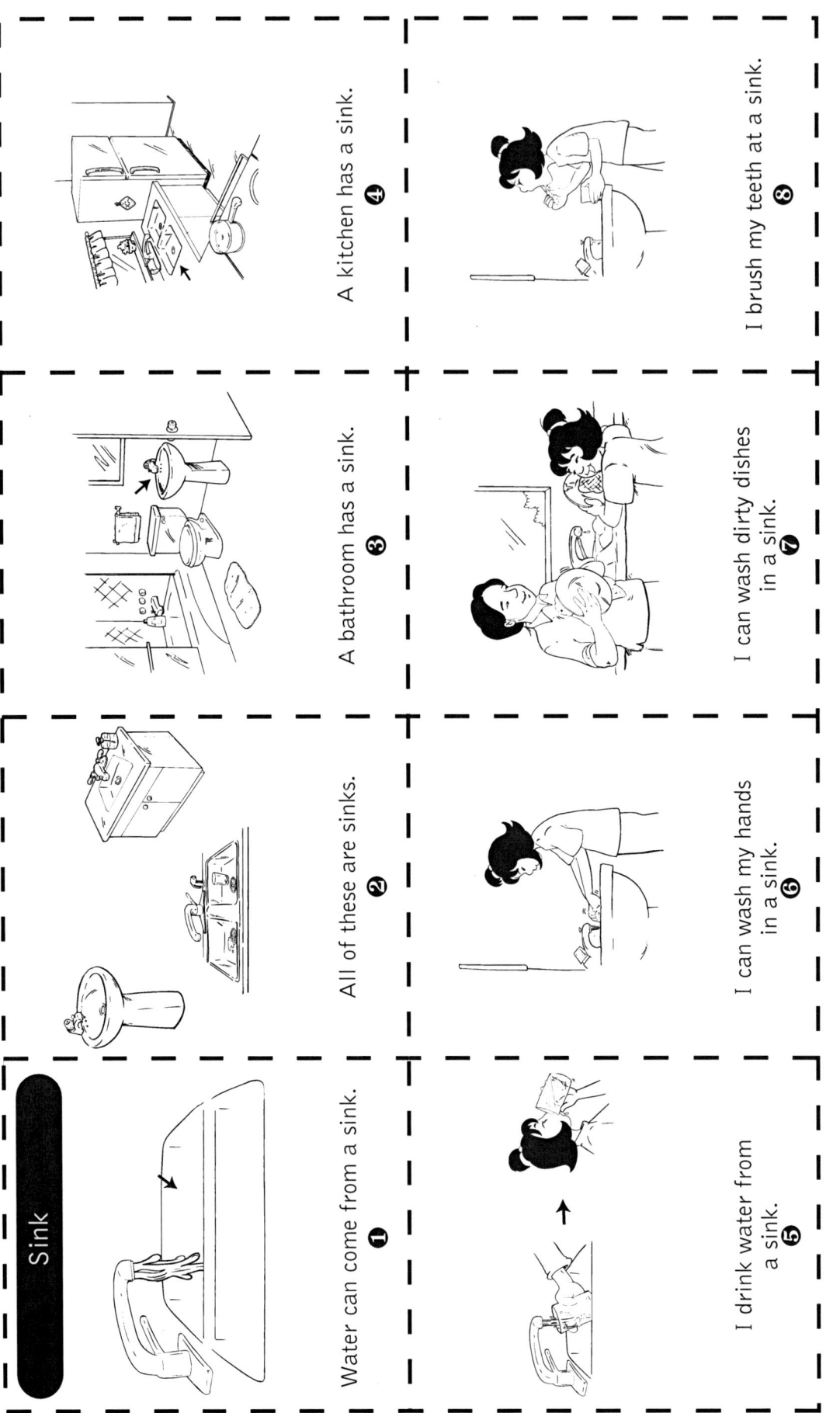

Sink

① Water can come from a sink.

② All of these are sinks.

③ A bathroom has a sink.

④ A kitchen has a sink.

⑤ I drink water from a sink.

⑥ I can wash my hands in a sink.

⑦ I can wash dirty dishes in a sink.

⑧ I brush my teeth at a sink.

Toilet

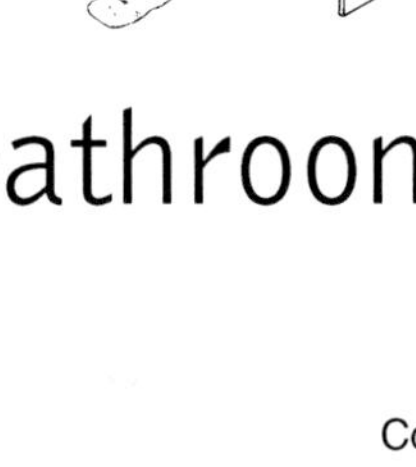

A toilet is in a bathroom.

Toilet

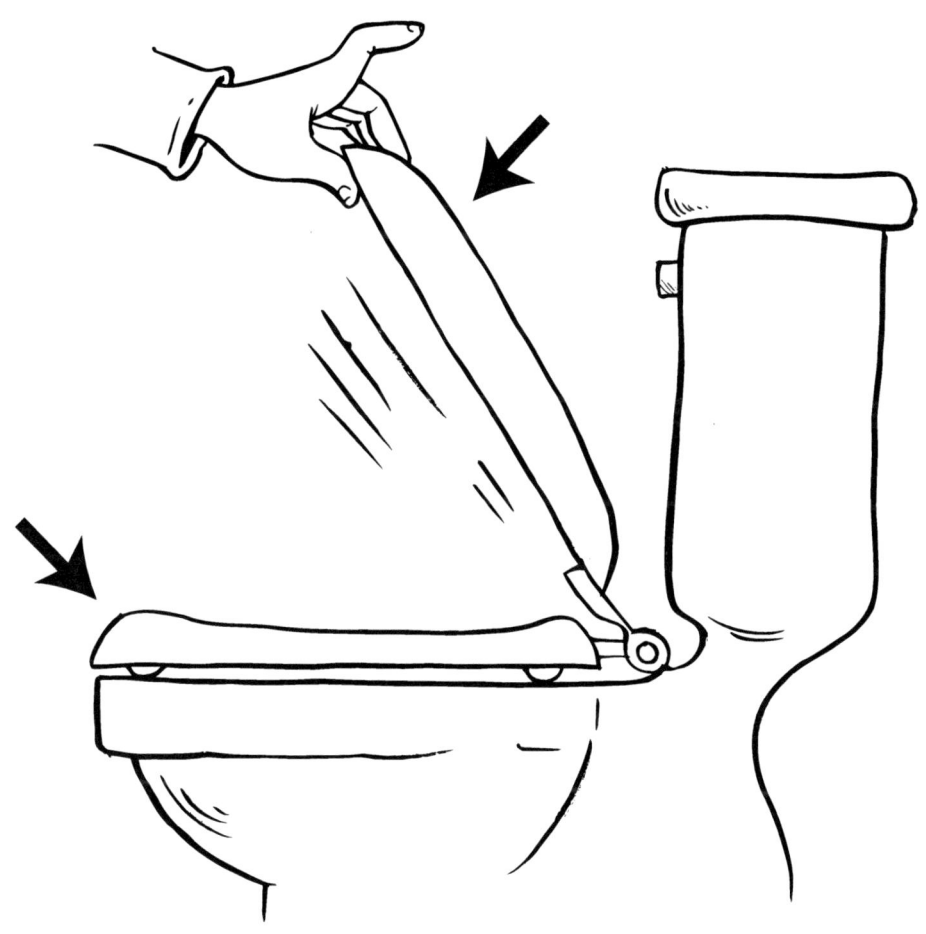

  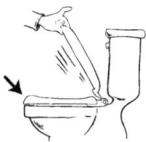

A toilet has a lid and a seat.

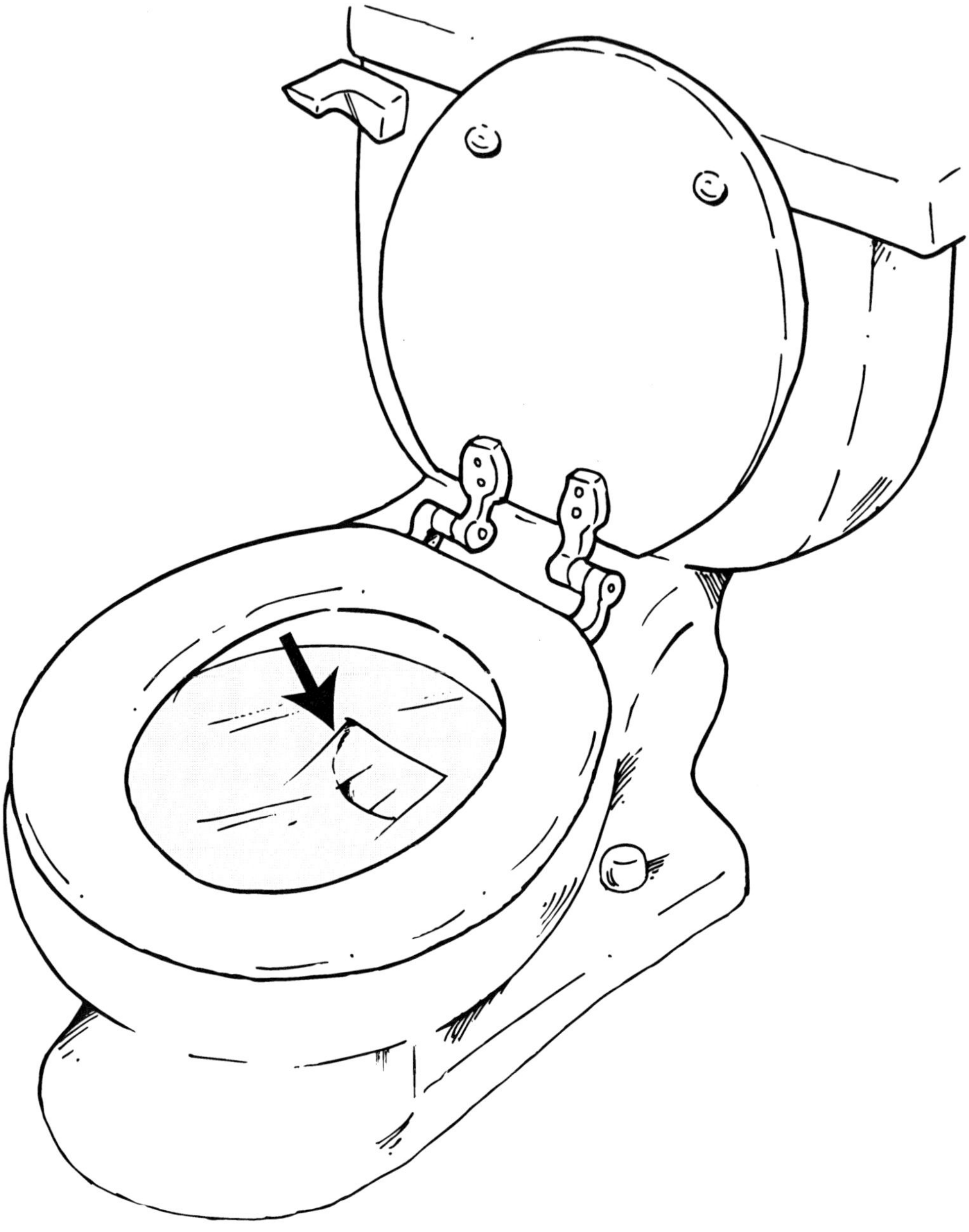

A toilet has water in it.

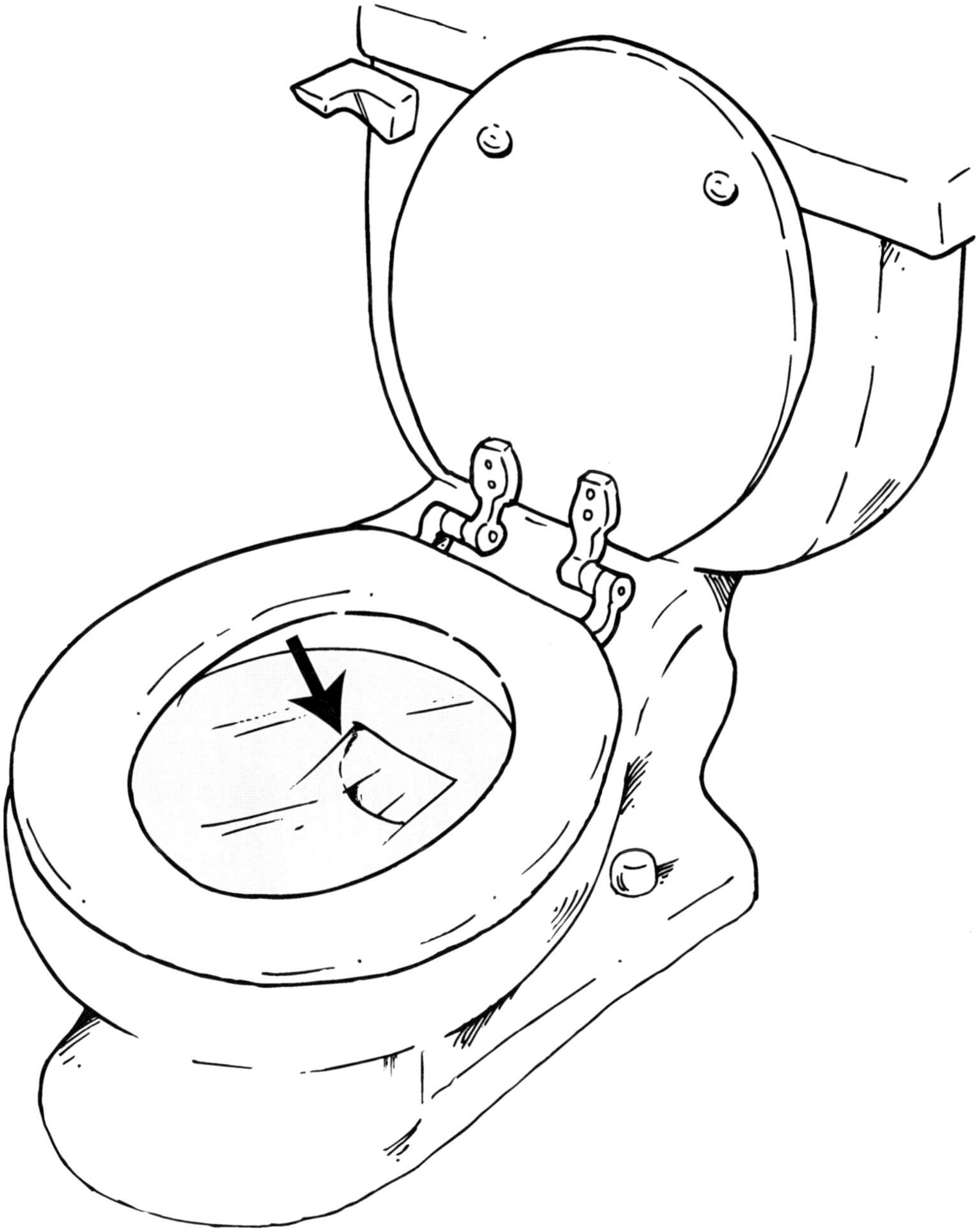

Pee and poop go in a toilet.

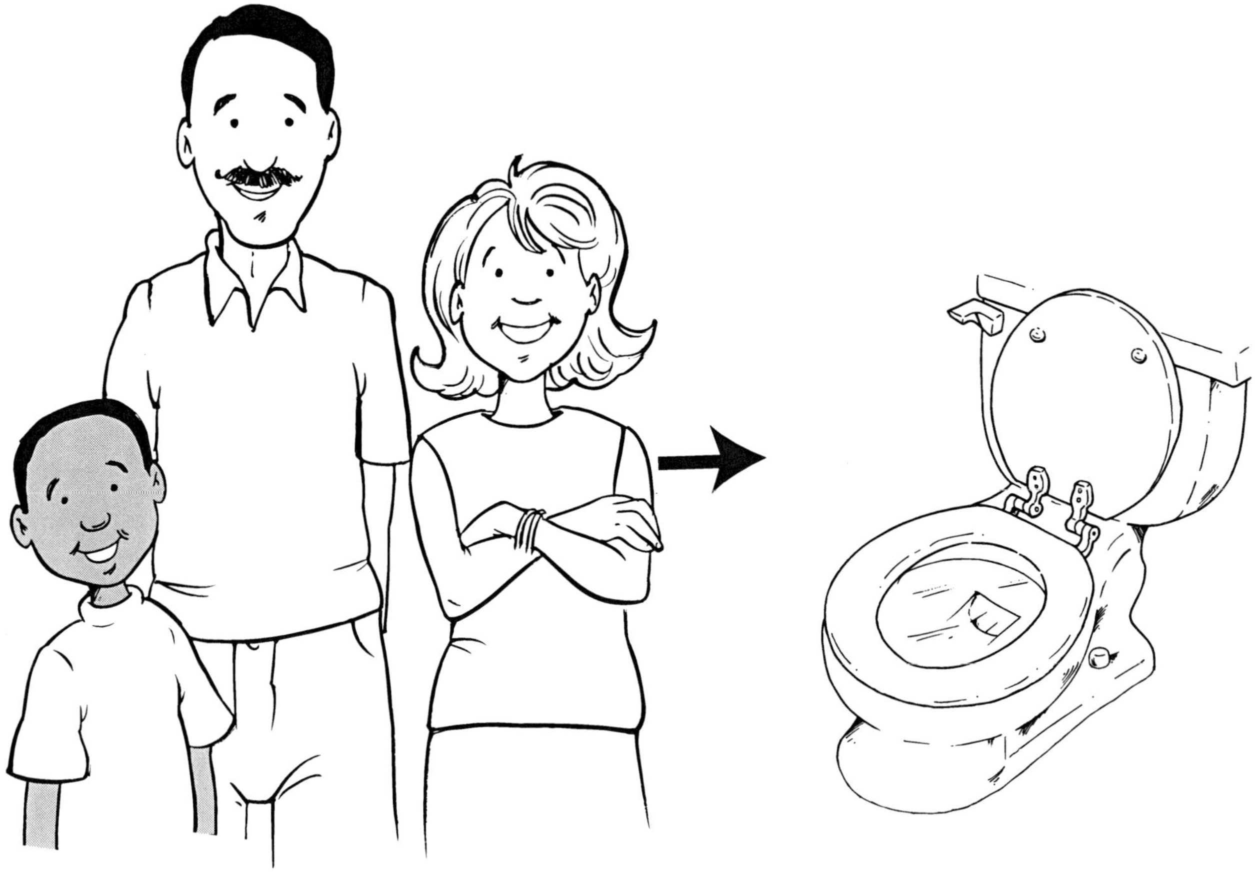

Everyone uses a toilet.

Girls sit on a toilet.

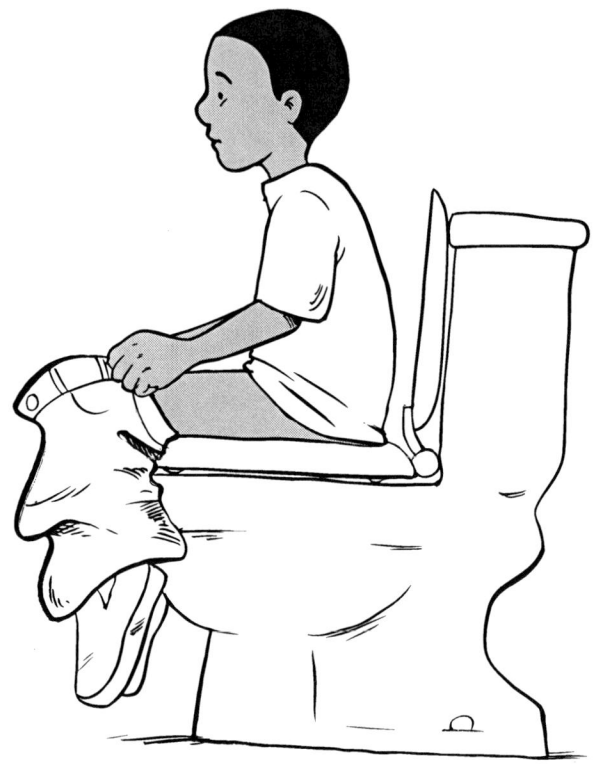

Boys stand at or sit on a toilet.

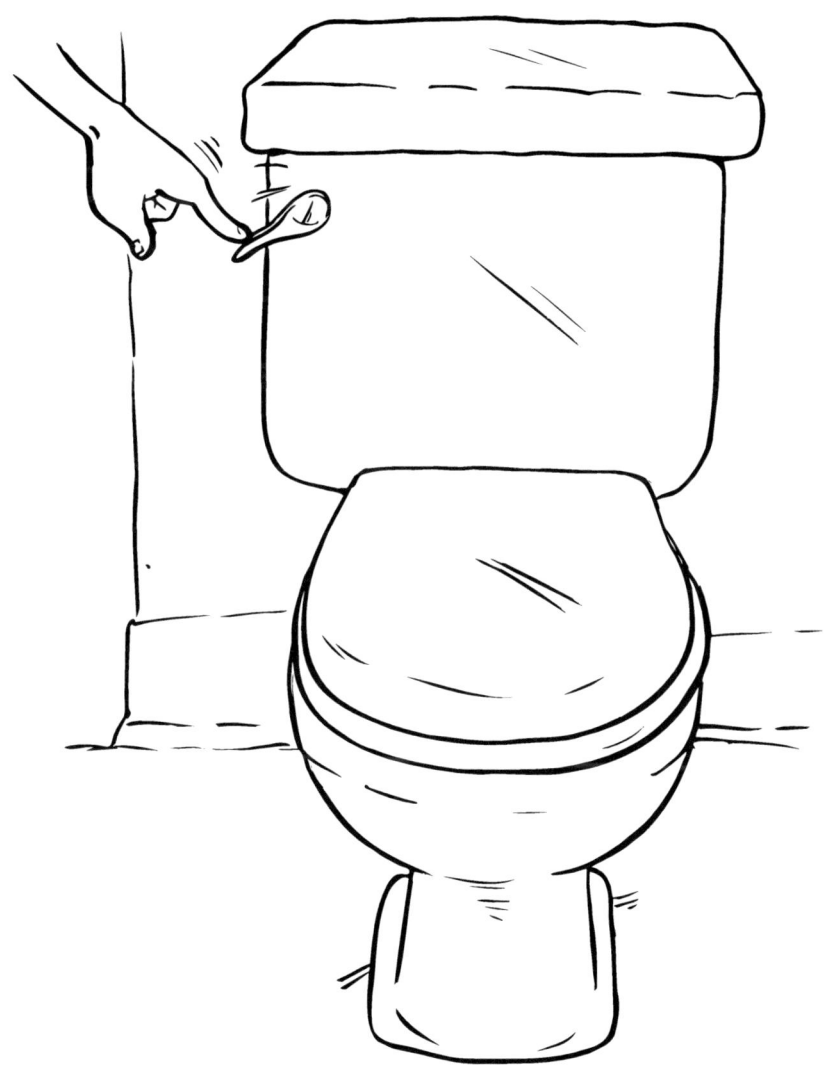

  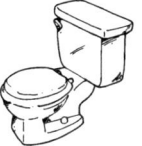

I can flush the toilet.

Concept: Toilet

Yes-No Questions

1. Is a toilet in the kitchen?
2. Does a toilet have a lid?
3. Does a toilet have a seat?
4. Do toys go in a toilet?
5. Do girls sit on a toilet?
6. Do boys stand on top of a toilet?
7. Does a toilet flush?
8. Do you use a toilet?
9. Does everyone use a toilet?
10. Does a toilet have water in it?

Wh- and How Questions

1. Where is a toilet?
2. What does a toilet have?
3. What goes in a toilet?
4. Who sits on a toilet?
5. Who stands in front of a toilet?
6. How do you flush a toilet?
7. Who uses a toilet?
8. Who can stand at or sit on a toilet?
9. Why do we have toilets?
10. When do we flush toilets?

Toilet Generalization Page

Circle the toilets. Put an X on each picture that is not a toilet.

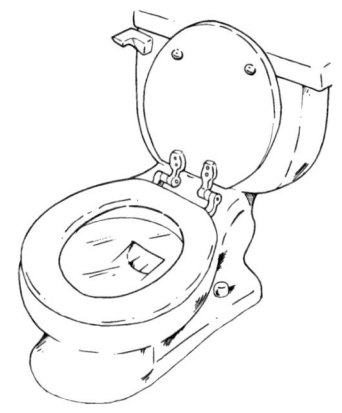

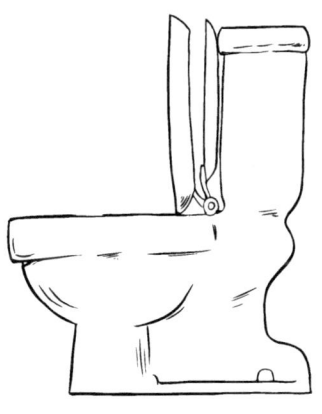
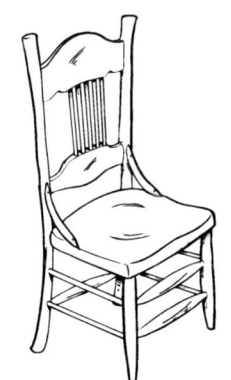
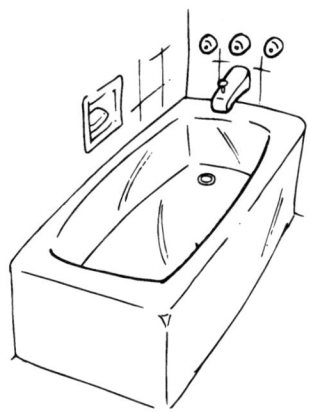
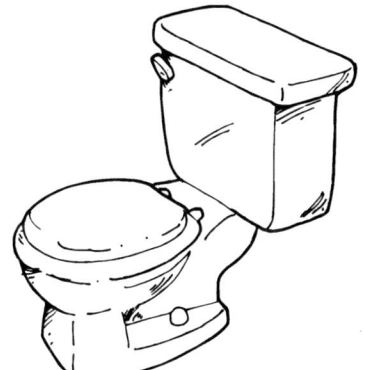

Toilet Mini-Book

Copy this page. Cut apart the boxes on the dotted lines. Put the story in order to make a little book and staple.

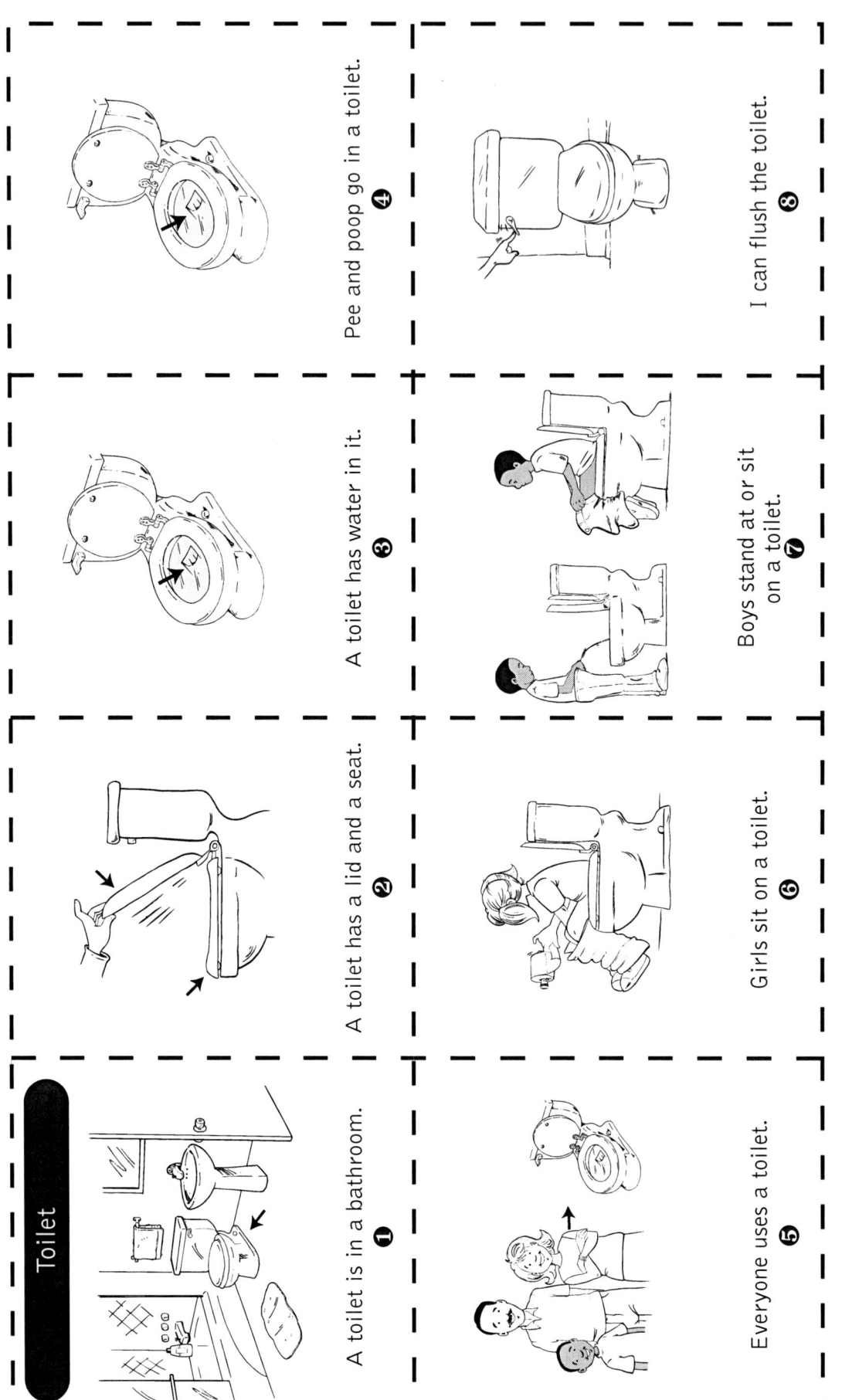

① A toilet is in a bathroom.

② A toilet has a lid and a seat.

③ A toilet has water in it.

④ Pee and poop go in a toilet.

⑤ Everyone uses a toilet.

⑥ Girls sit on a toilet.

⑦ Boys stand at or sit on a toilet.

⑧ I can flush the toilet.

Toilet
Concept Development

68

Copyright © 2001 LinguiSystems, Inc.

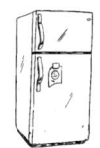 

A refrigerator is in a kitchen.

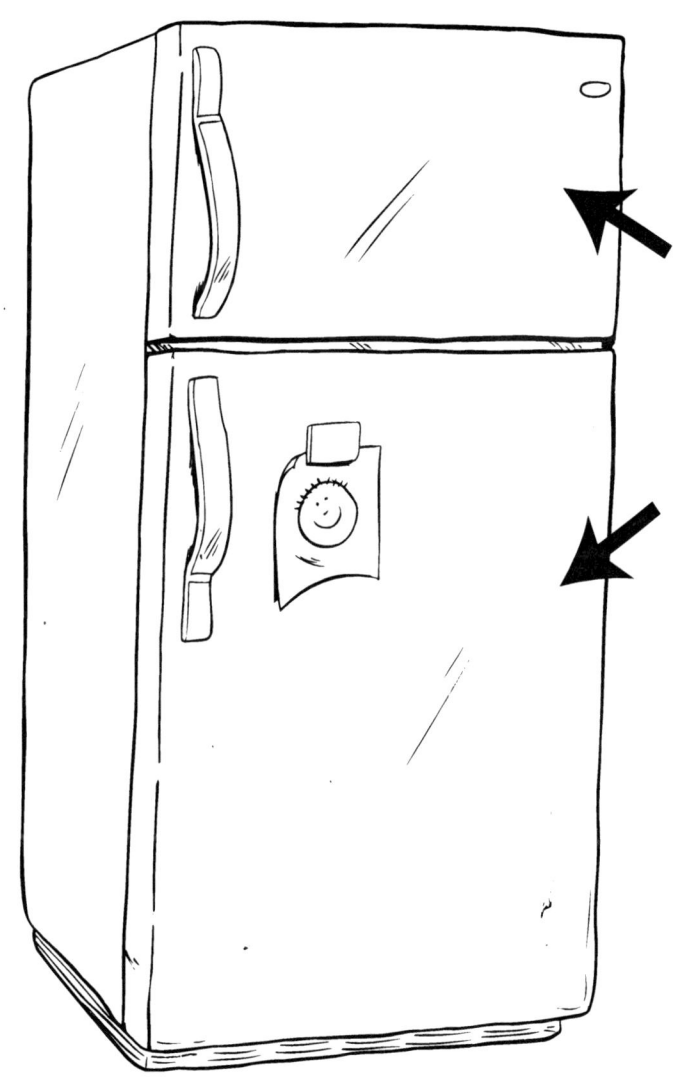

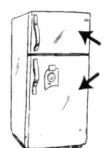

A refrigerator has doors.

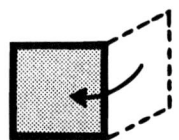  •

I close the refrigerator door after I get out the food.

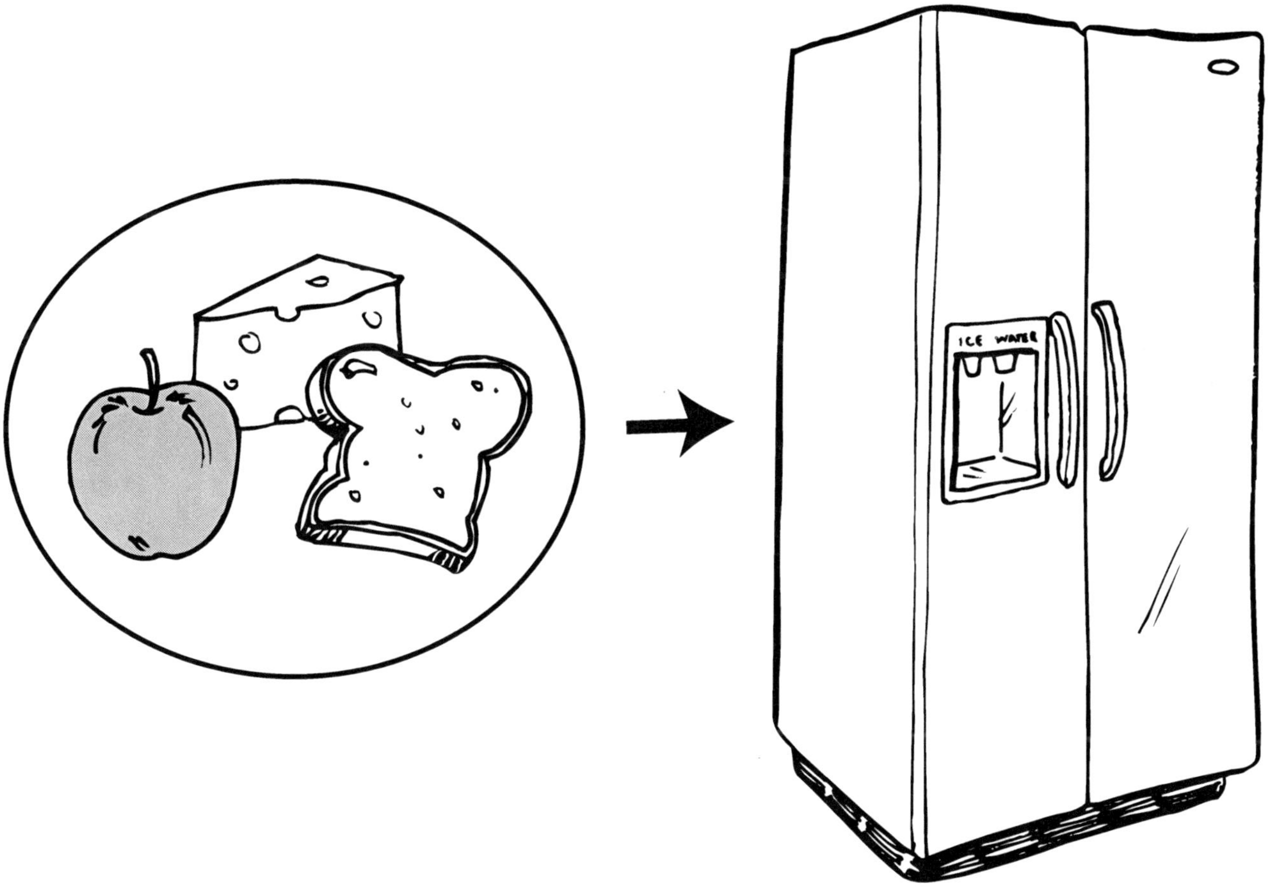

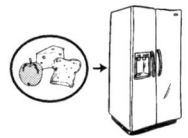

We keep food in a refrigerator.

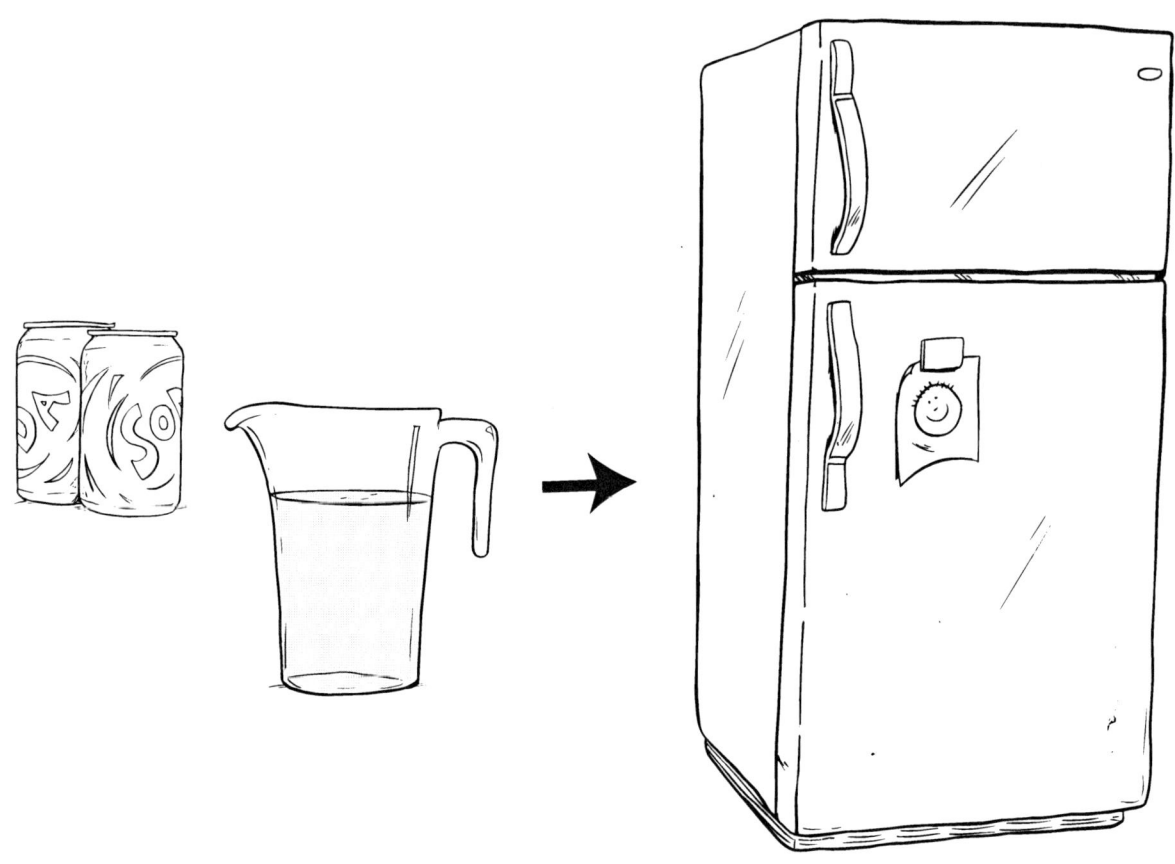

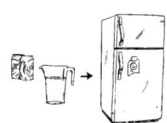

We keep drinks in a refrigerator.

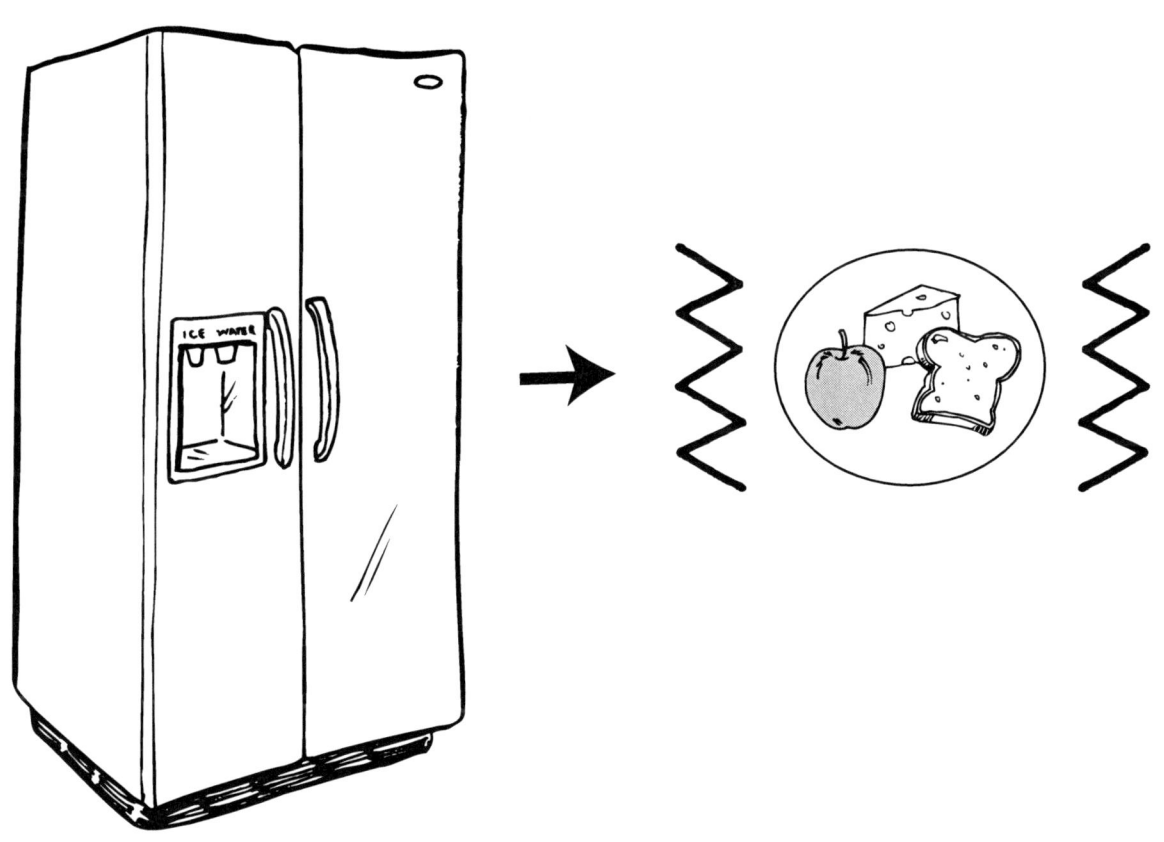

A refrigerator keeps food cold.

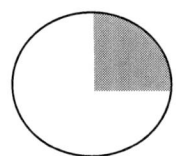 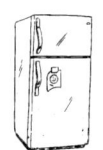 

Part of the refrigerator is called a freezer.

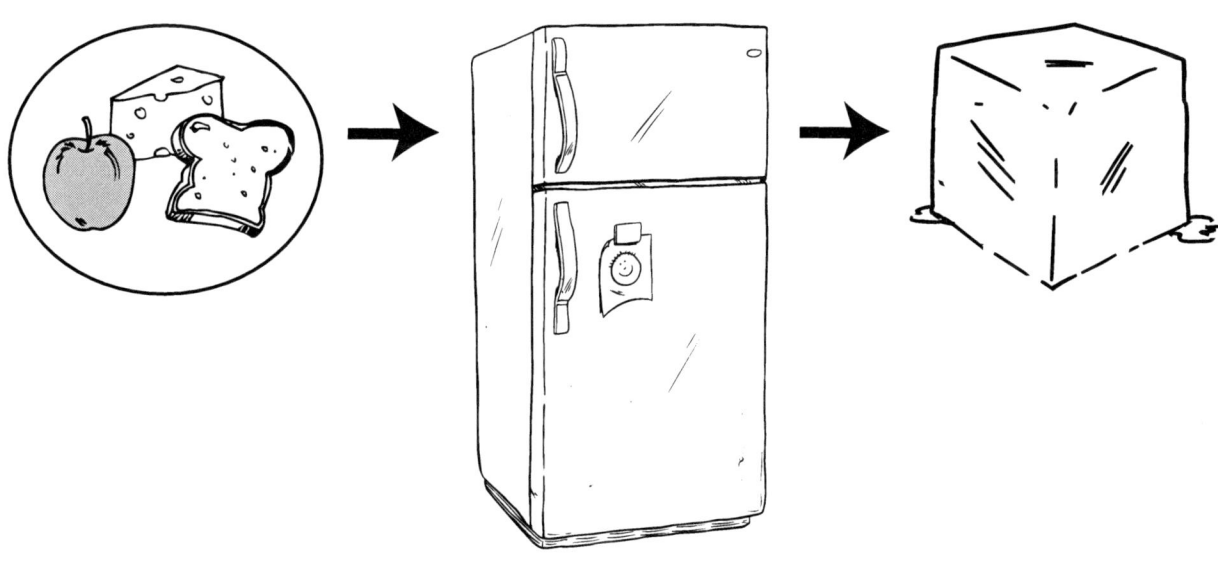

 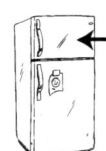 

Food in the freezer is frozen.

Concept: Refrigerator

Yes-No Questions

1. Is a refrigerator in a bedroom?
2. Is a refrigerator in a kitchen?
3. Does a refrigerator have windows?
4. Do we keep food in a refrigerator?
5. Do we keep toys in a refrigerator?
6. Do we keep drinks in a refrigerator?
7. Does a refrigerator keep food cold?
8. Is part of a refrigerator called an oven?
9. Is part of a refrigerator called a freezer?
10. Is food in the freezer frozen?

Wh- and How Questions

1. Where is a refrigerator?
2. What do we close on a refrigerator?
3. Where do we keep cold food?
4. Where do we keep drinks?
5. What do we call part of the refrigerator?
6. Where is frozen food?
7. Why do we keep food and drinks in the refrigerator?
8. Why do we keep refrigerator doors shut?
9. How do you keep food cold?
10. Who has a refrigerator?

Refrigerator Generalization Page

Circle the refrigerators. Put an X on each picture that does not show a refrigerator.

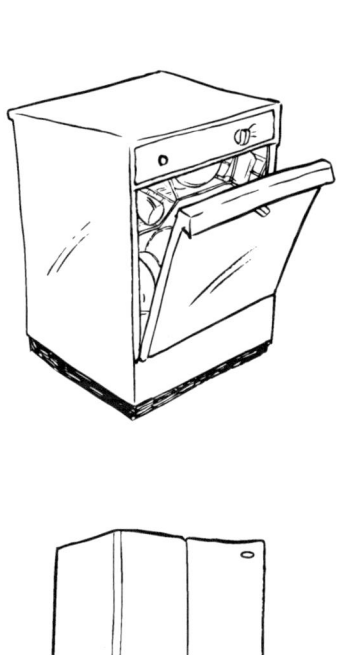

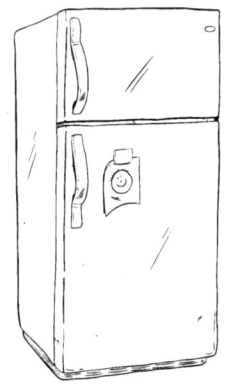

Refrigerator Mini-Book

Copy this page. Cut apart the boxes on the dotted lines. Put the story in order to make a little book and staple.

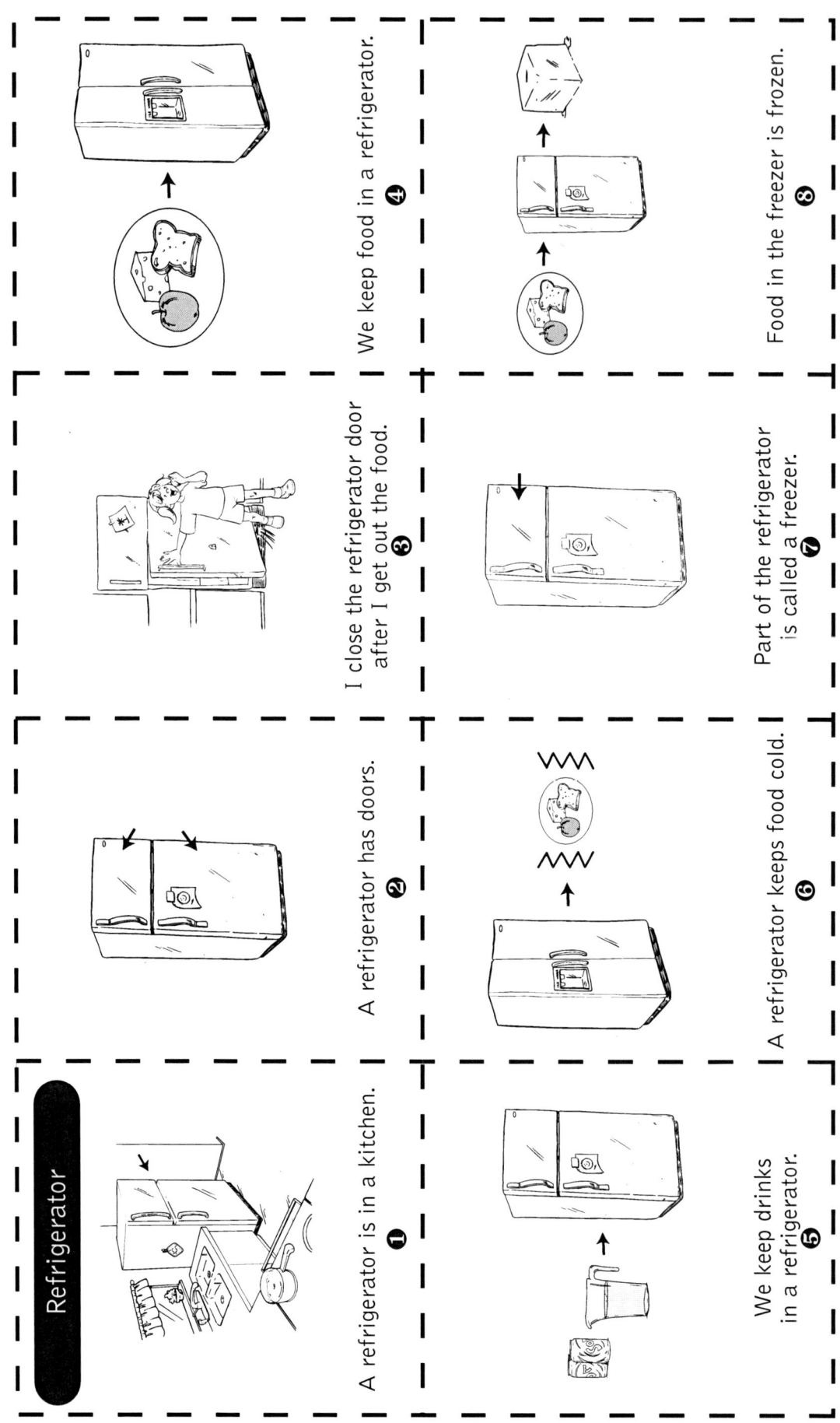

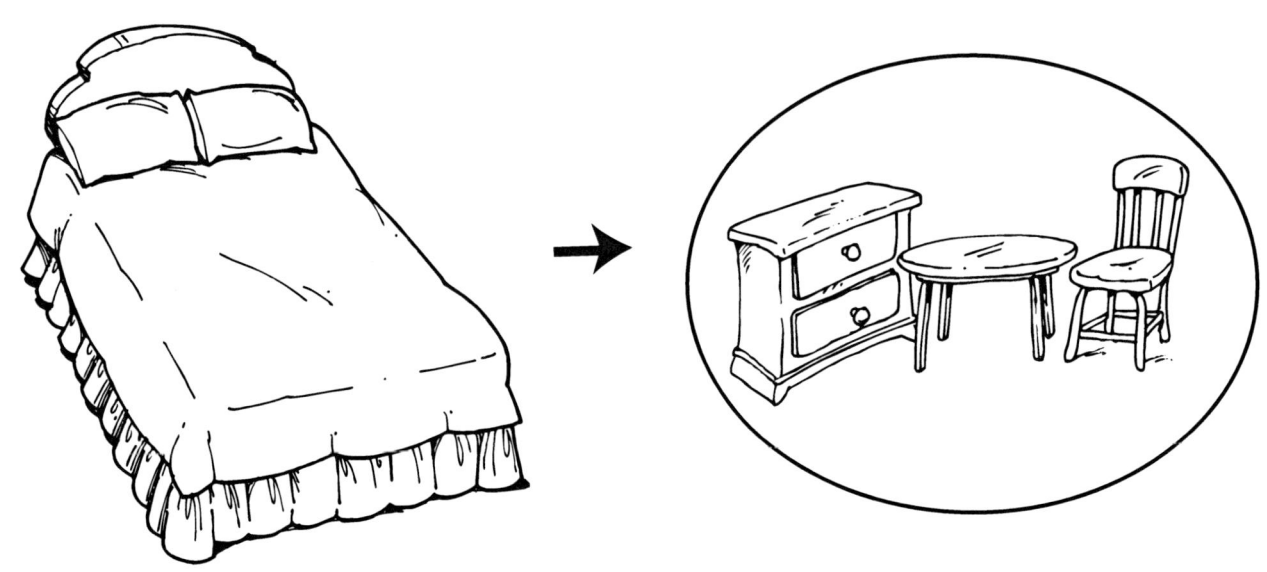

A bed is a piece of furniture.

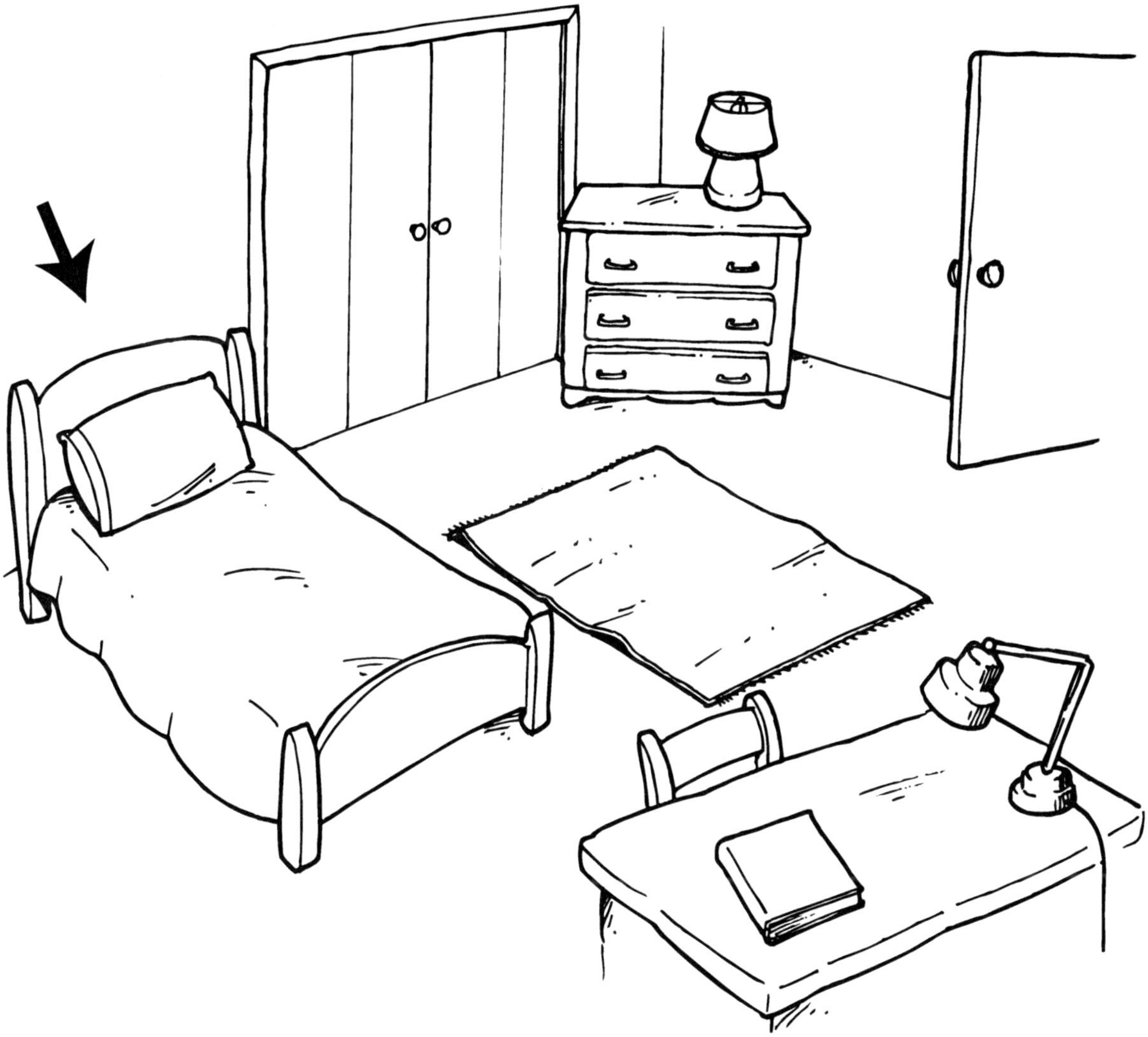

 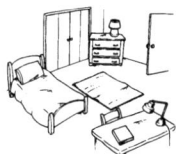

A bed is in a bedroom.

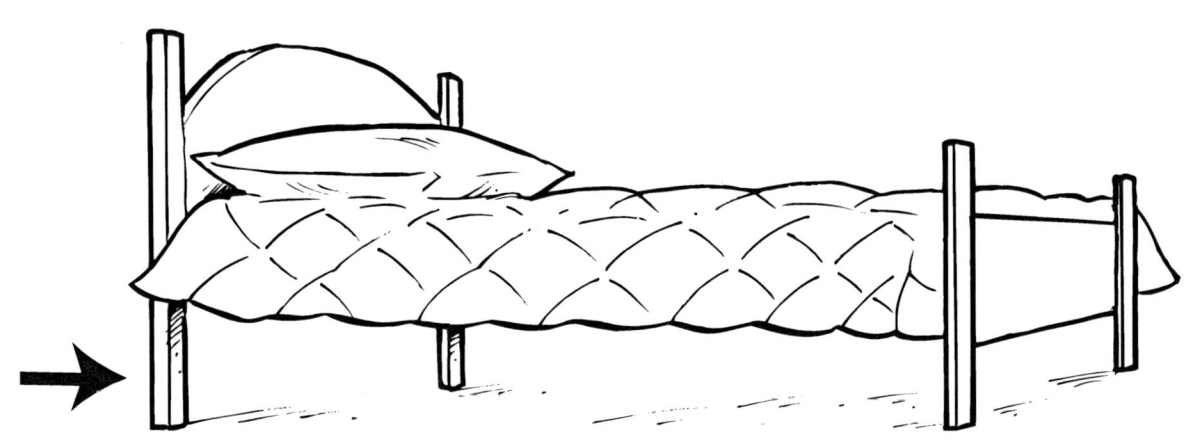

 4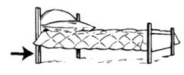

A bed has four legs.

A bed has a pillow.

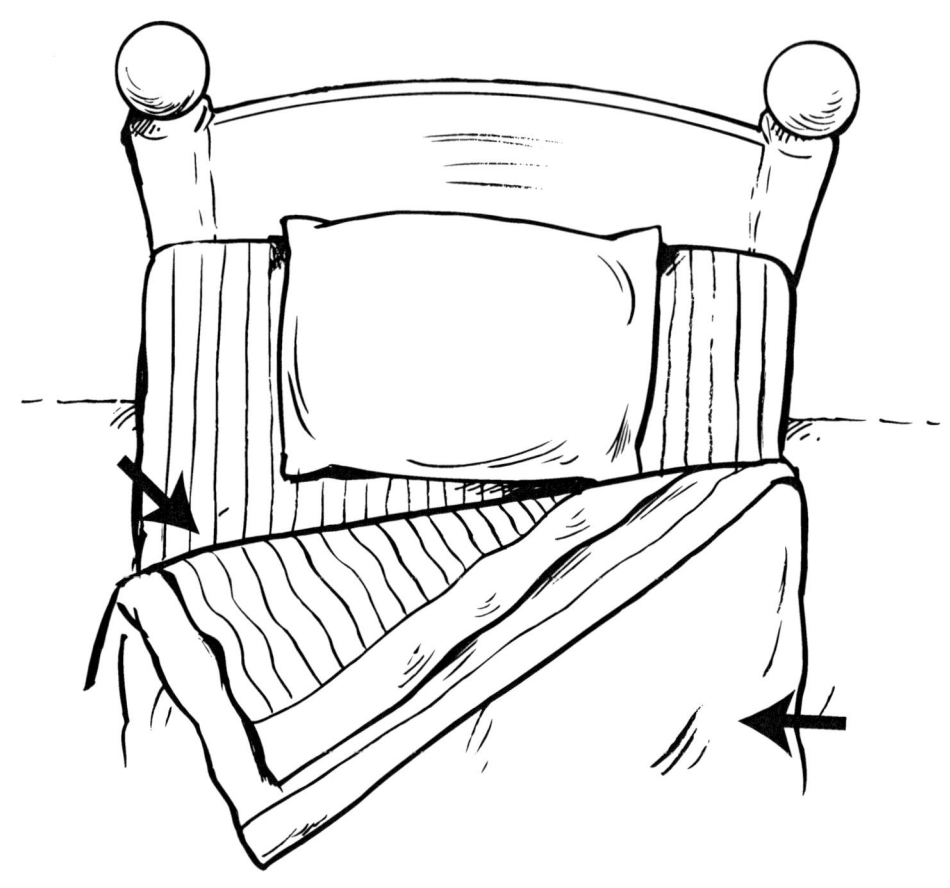

A bed has sheets and blankets.

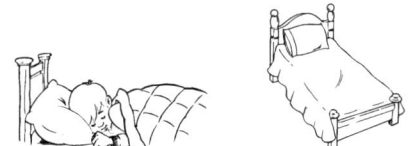

I sleep in a bed.

I can take a nap in bed.

 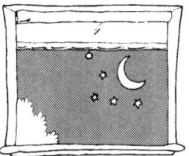

I go to bed at night.

Concept: Bed

Yes-No Questions

1. Is a bed a piece of furniture?
2. Is a bed in the bathroom?
3. Is a bed in the bedroom?
4. Does a bed have four legs?
5. Does a bed have a pillow?
6. Do we draw pictures in bed?
7. Do we sometimes take naps in a bed?
8. Do we use a bed at night?
9. Do you have a bed?
10. Do you sleep in a bed?

Wh- and How Questions

1. Where are sheets?
2. Where are pillows?
3. What do you do in a bed?
4. How many legs does a bed have?
5. When do we sleep in a bed?
6. Who sleeps in a bed?
7. What is a bed?
8. Where can you take a nap?
9. Why do we have beds?
10. Why do we have pillows?

Bed Generalization Page

Circle the beds. Put an X on each picture that is not a bed.

Bed Mini-Book

Copy this page. Cut apart the boxes on the dotted lines. Put the story in order to make a little book and staple.

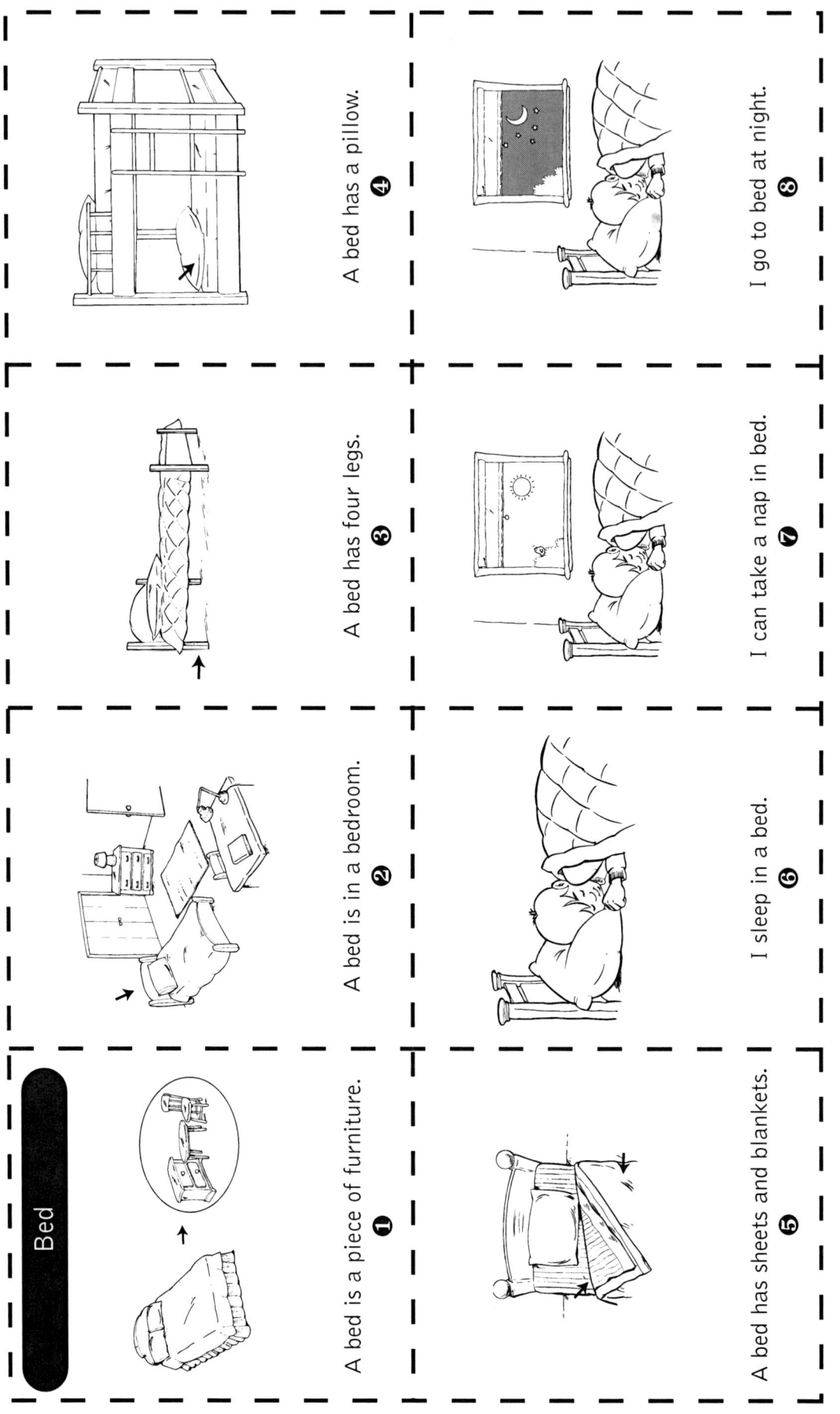

Bed

A bed is a piece of furniture. ❶

A bed is in a bedroom. ❷

A bed has four legs. ❸

A bed has a pillow. ❹

A bed has sheets and blankets. ❺

I sleep in a bed. ❻

I can take a nap in bed. ❼

I go to bed at night. ❽

A lamp makes light.

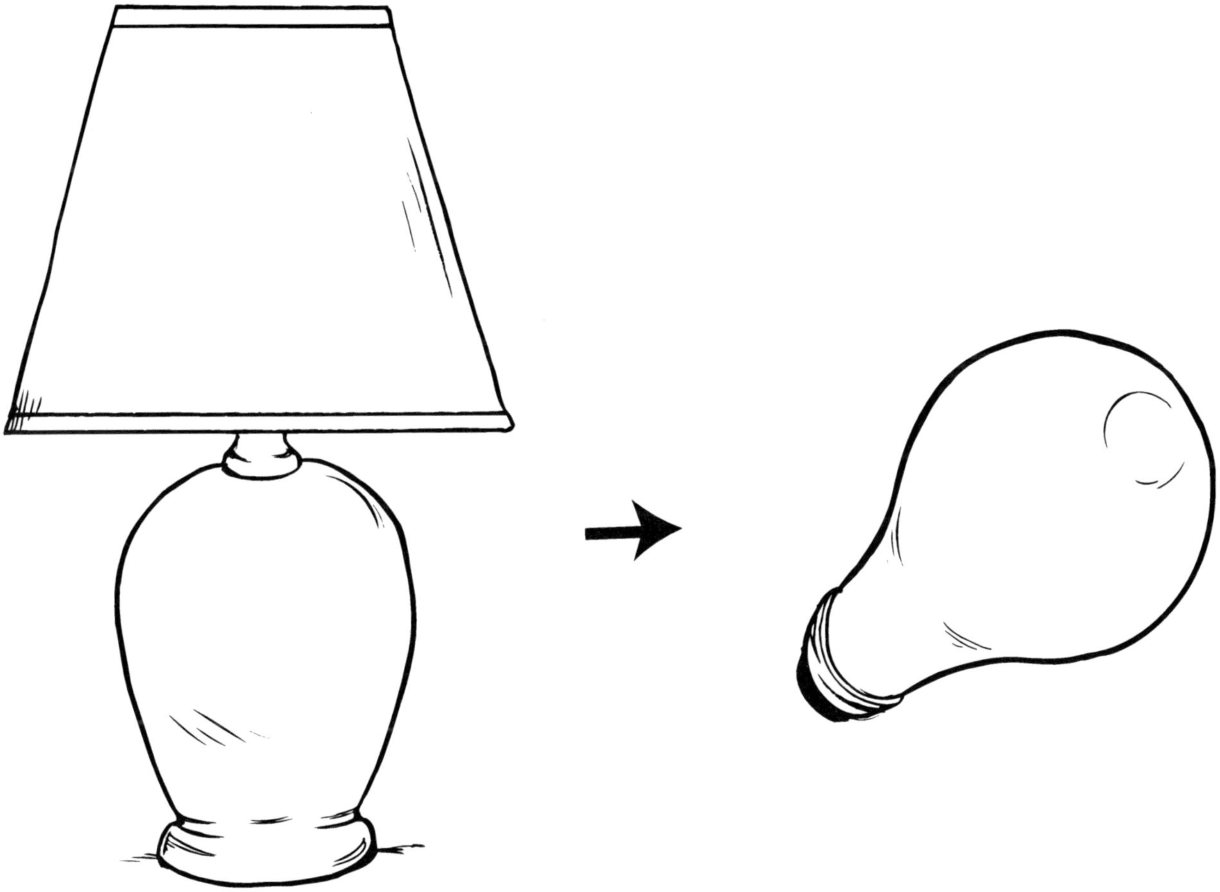

A lamp has a light bulb.

A lamp has a cord.

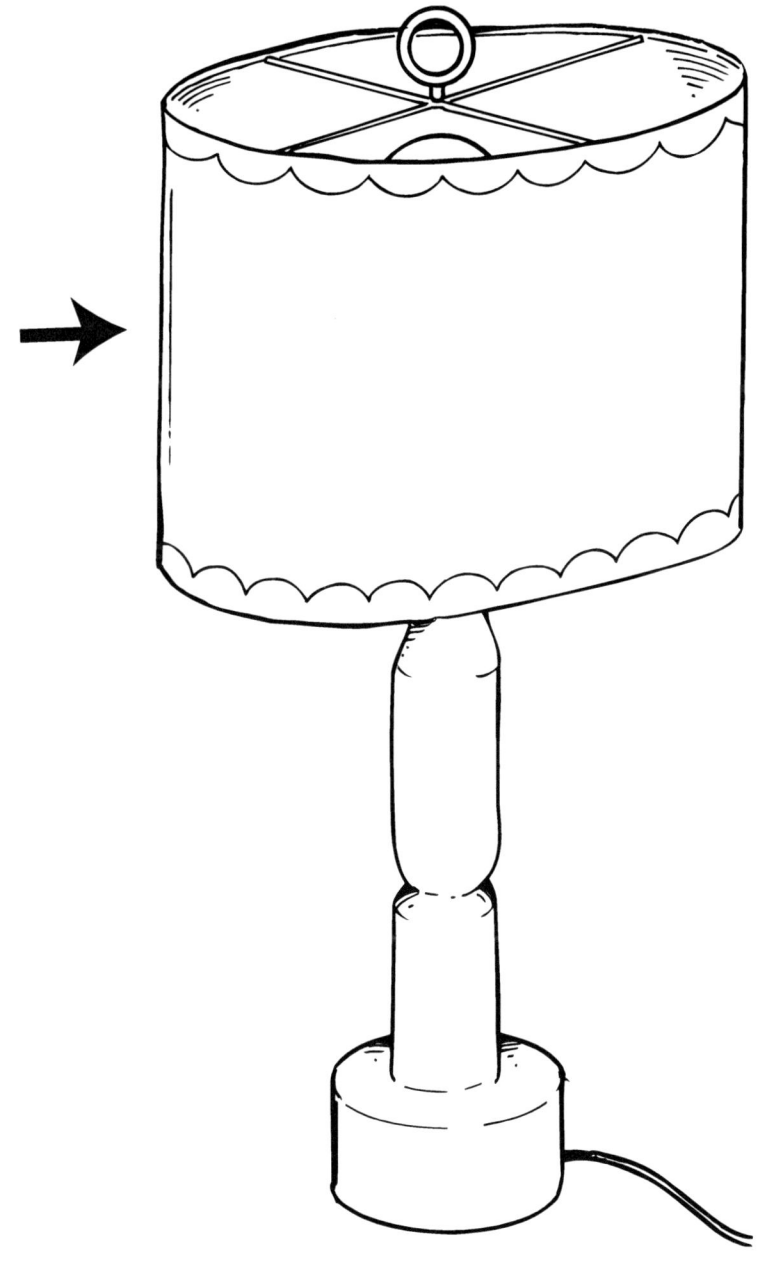

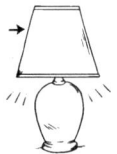

A lamp has a shade.

A lamp can go on a table or on the floor.

All of these are lamps.

Lamp

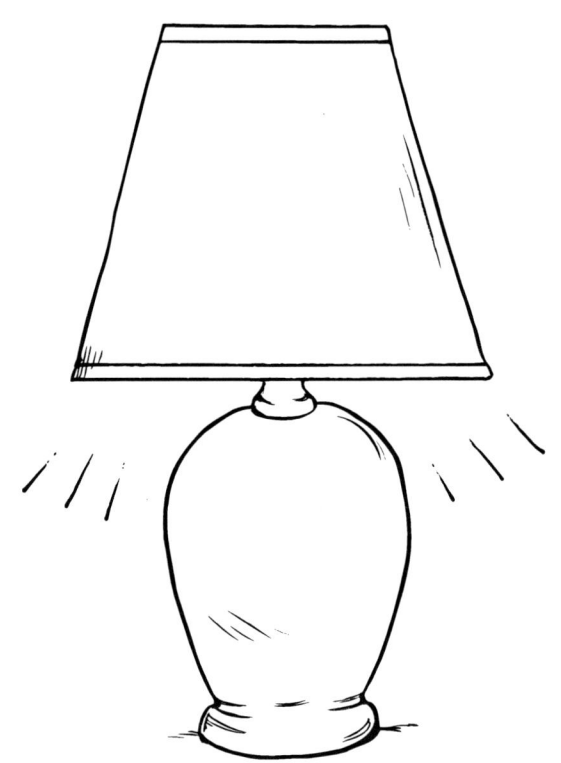 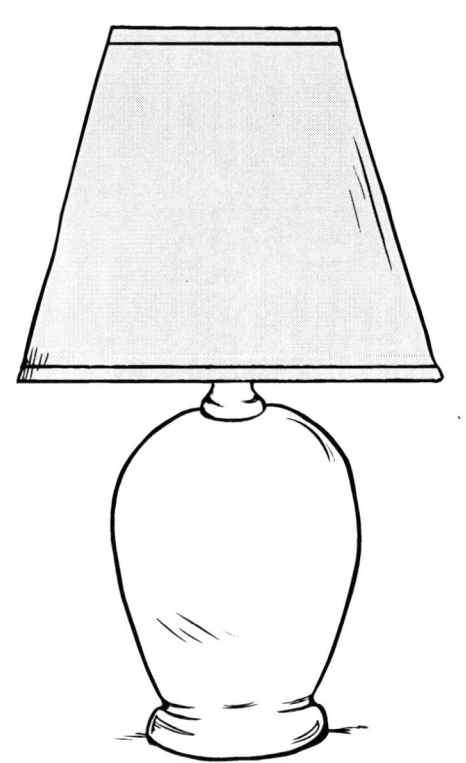

I can turn a lamp on or off.

A lamp helps me see when it is dark.

Concept: Lamp

Yes-No Questions

1. Does a lamp make light?
2. Does a lamp have shoes?
3. Does a lamp have a cord?
4. Can you turn off a lamp?
5. Can you turn on a lamp?
6. Do lamps have light bulbs?
7. Can a lamp sit on a table?
8. Can a lamp sit on a bed?
9. Can a lamp sit on the floor?
10. Does a lamp help you see?

Wh- and How Questions

1. What does a lamp make?
2. Where does a lamp sit?
3. Why does a lamp have a cord?
4. How do you turn on a lamp?
5. How do you turn off a lamp?
6. How does a lamp help you?
7. What has a light bulb?
8. When do you turn on a lamp?
9. Why do we have lamps?
10. What can you turn on or off?

Lamp Generalization Page

Circle the lamps. Put an X on each picture that is not a lamp.

Lamp
Concept Development

Lamp Mini-Book

Copy this page. Cut apart the boxes on the dotted lines. Put the story in order to make a little book and staple.

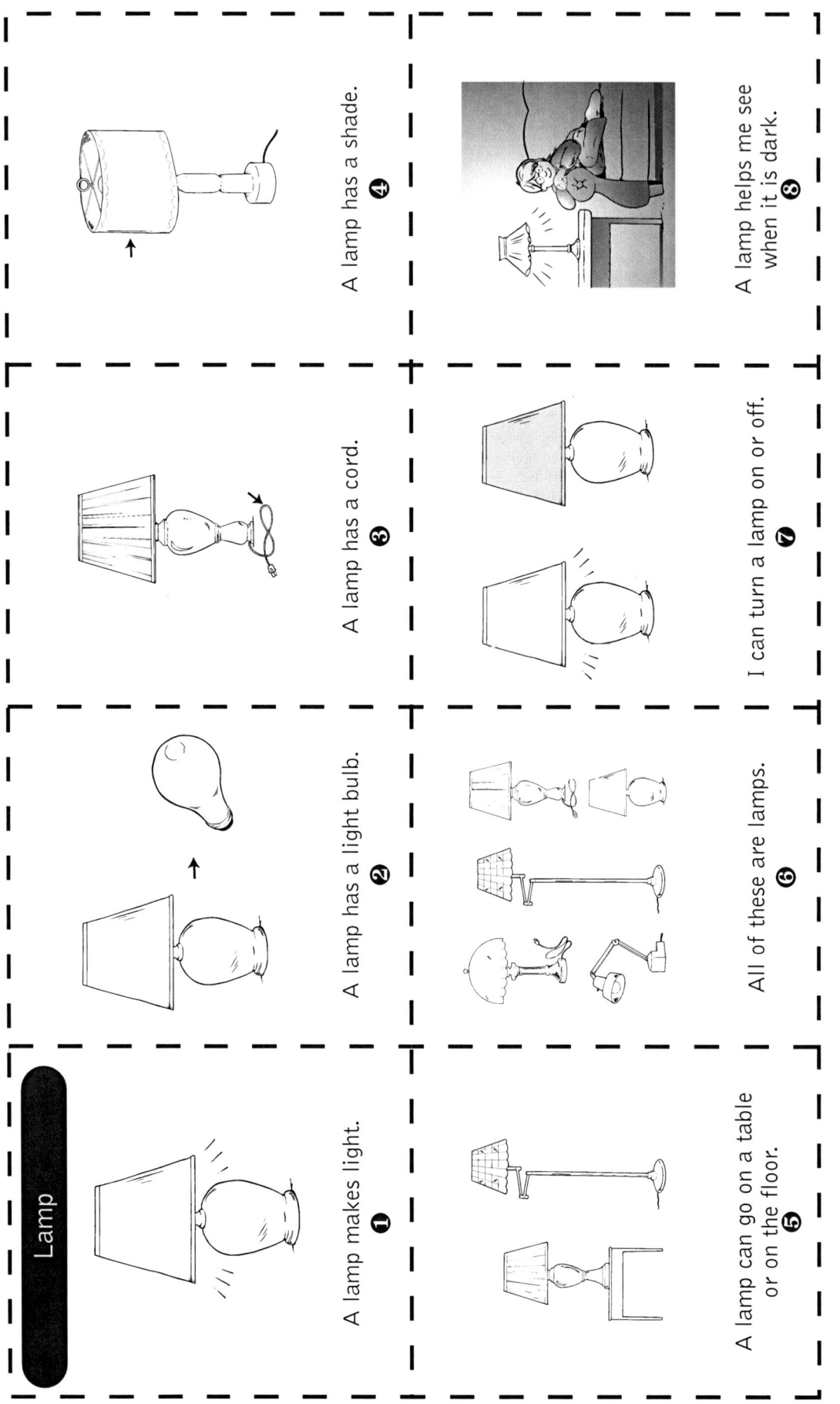

Telephone

   1 2 3   A B C

A telephone has buttons with numbers and letters.

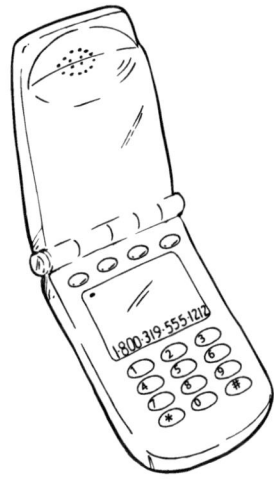
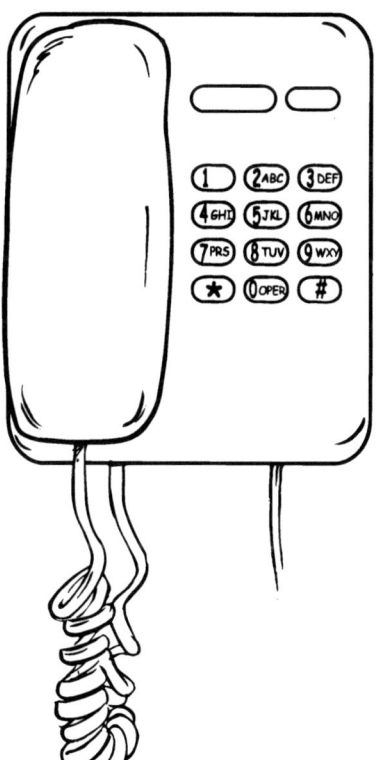

All of these are telephones.

I can dial the telephone to call people.

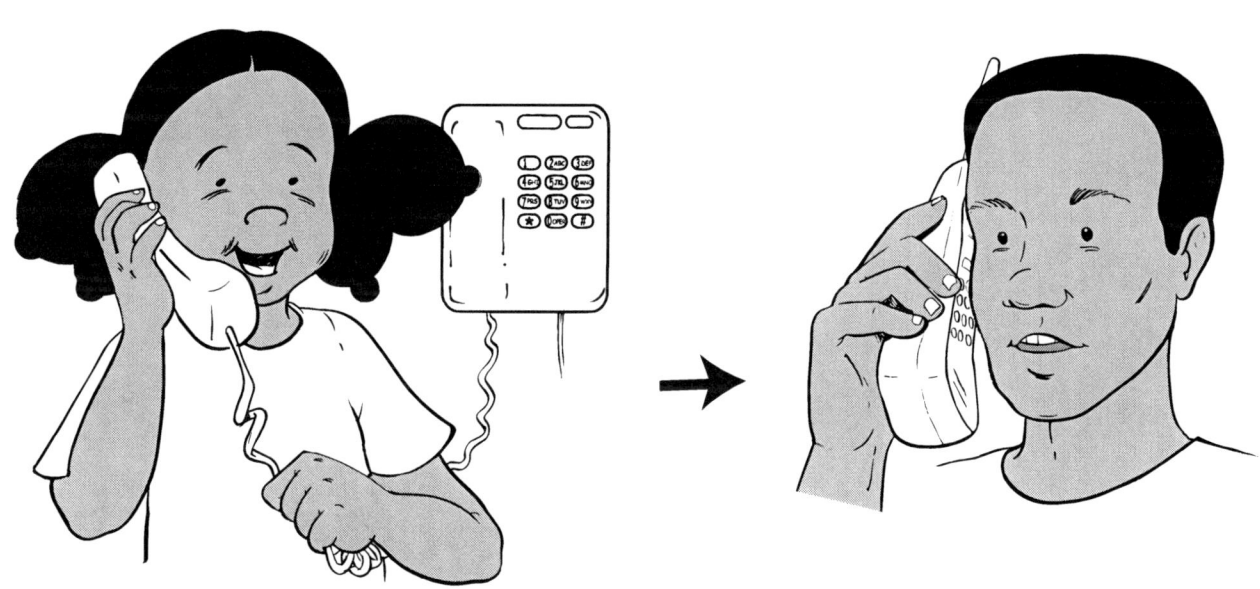

I can talk to people on the telephone.

A telephone rings.

I can answer the telephone.

I can say, "Hello!"

When I am finished talking I can say, "Good-bye."

Concept: Telephone

Yes-No Questions

1. Does a telephone ring?
2. Do people say "Hello" on the phone?
3. Do you throw a telephone?
4. Do you answer a telephone?
5. Does a telephone have pillows?
6. Does a telephone have buttons with numbers and letters?
7. Do you dial a telephone?
8. Do you say "Good-bye" before you hang up?
9. Do people sleep on a telephone?
10. Do you talk to people on a telephone?

Wh- and How Questions

1. What rings?
2. Who can answer a telephone?
3. What can you say on a telephone?
4. Who do you talk to on a telephone?
5. What do you do with a telephone?
6. How do you dial a telephone?
7. Where is a telephone?
8. What has buttons with numbers and letters?
9. When do you say "Good-bye" on a telephone?
10. How do you answer a telephone?

Telephone Generalization Page

Circle the telephones. Put an X on each picture that is not a telephone.

Telephone Mini-Book

Copy this page. Cut apart the boxes on the dotted lines. Put the story in order to make a little book and staple.

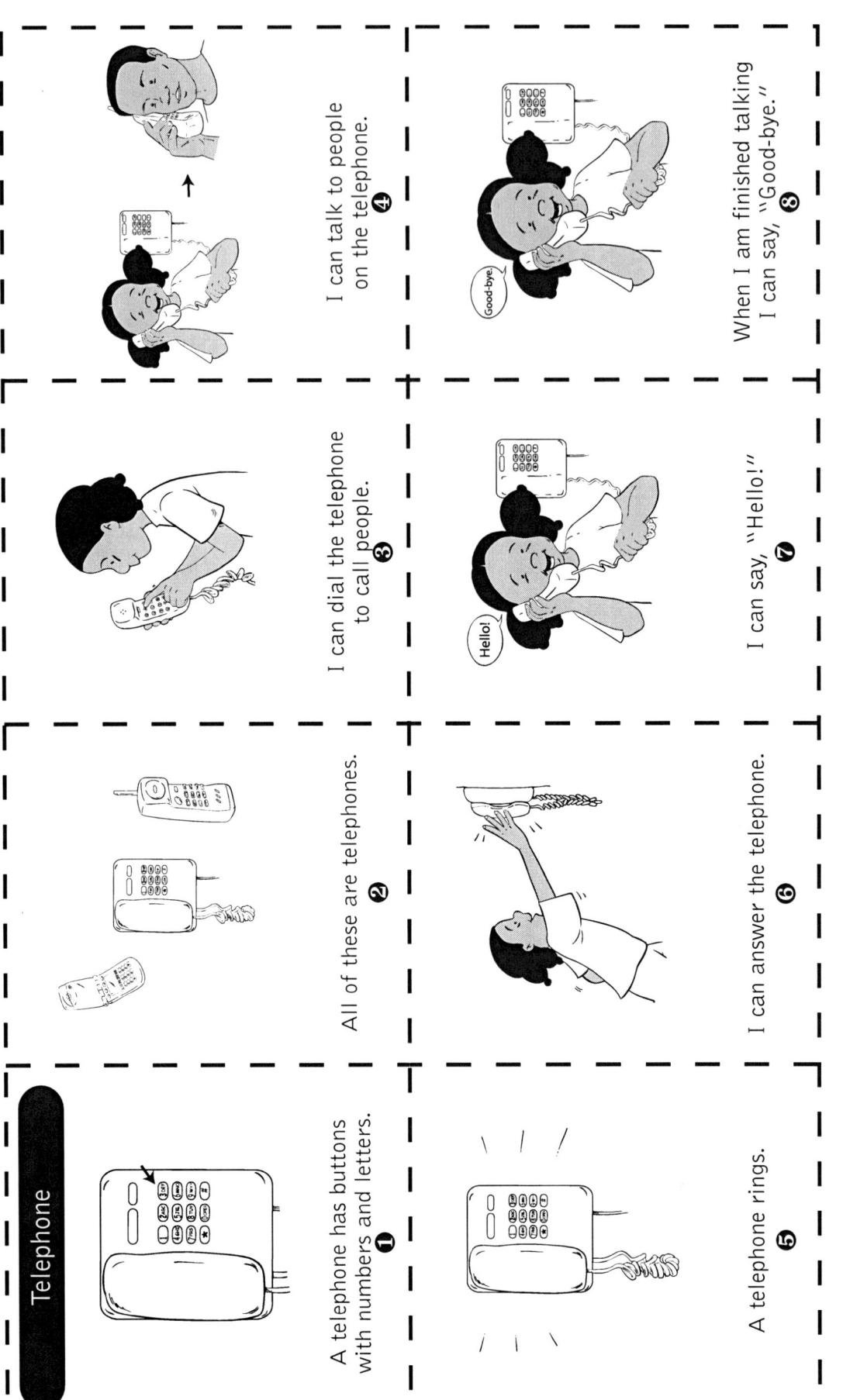

Telephone
Concept Development

Copyright © 2001 LinguiSystems, Inc.

 television

This is called a TV or a television.

I watch television.

A television has a screen.

I can turn on the television.

I can change channels.

I can make the TV loud or quiet.

I like to watch cartoons on TV.

When I am finished, I can turn off the TV.

Concept: Television

Yes-No Questions

1. Do we talk on TVs?
2. Do we watch shows on TV?
3. Does a television have pages?
4. Does a television have a screen?
5. Can we change channels on a TV?
6. Can we make a TV loud?
7. Can we make a TV quiet?
8. Do we leave the TV on when the show is finished?
9. Do you like to watch TV?
10. Do you like cartoons on TV?

Wh- and How Questions

1. What do we do with a TV?
2. Where is a TV?
3. How do we change channels?
4. How do you turn on the TV?
5. How do you make the TV louder?
6. What do you like to watch on TV?
7. What has a screen?
8. When do you turn off the TV?
9. Who watches TV?
10. Who can turn the TV on or off?

Television Generalization Page

Circle the televisions. Put an X on each picture that is not a television.

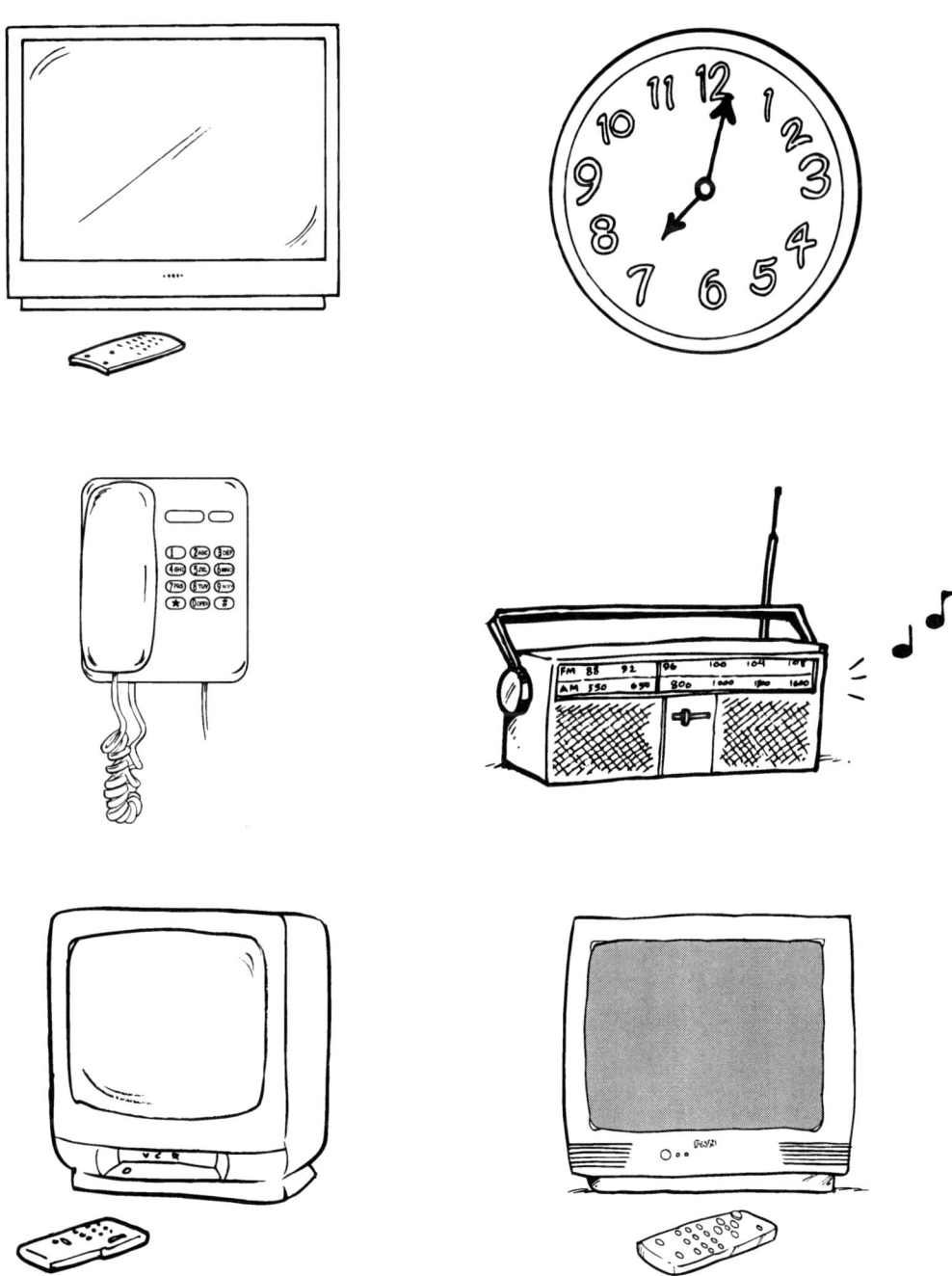

Television Mini-Book

Copy this page. Cut apart the boxes on the dotted lines. Put the story in order to make a little book and staple.

Television	I watch television. ❷	A television has a screen. ❸	I can turn on the television. ❹
This is called a TV or a television. ❶	I can make the TV loud or quiet. ❻	I like to watch cartoons on TV. ❼	When I am finished, I can turn off the TV. ❽
I can change channels. ❺			

Television
Concept Development

Copyright © 2001 LinguiSystems, Inc.

Extension Activity

Cut out the household items below and on page 130. Look at the rooms on pages 131-135 and help the child decide where each picture goes. Then glue or tape it in place.

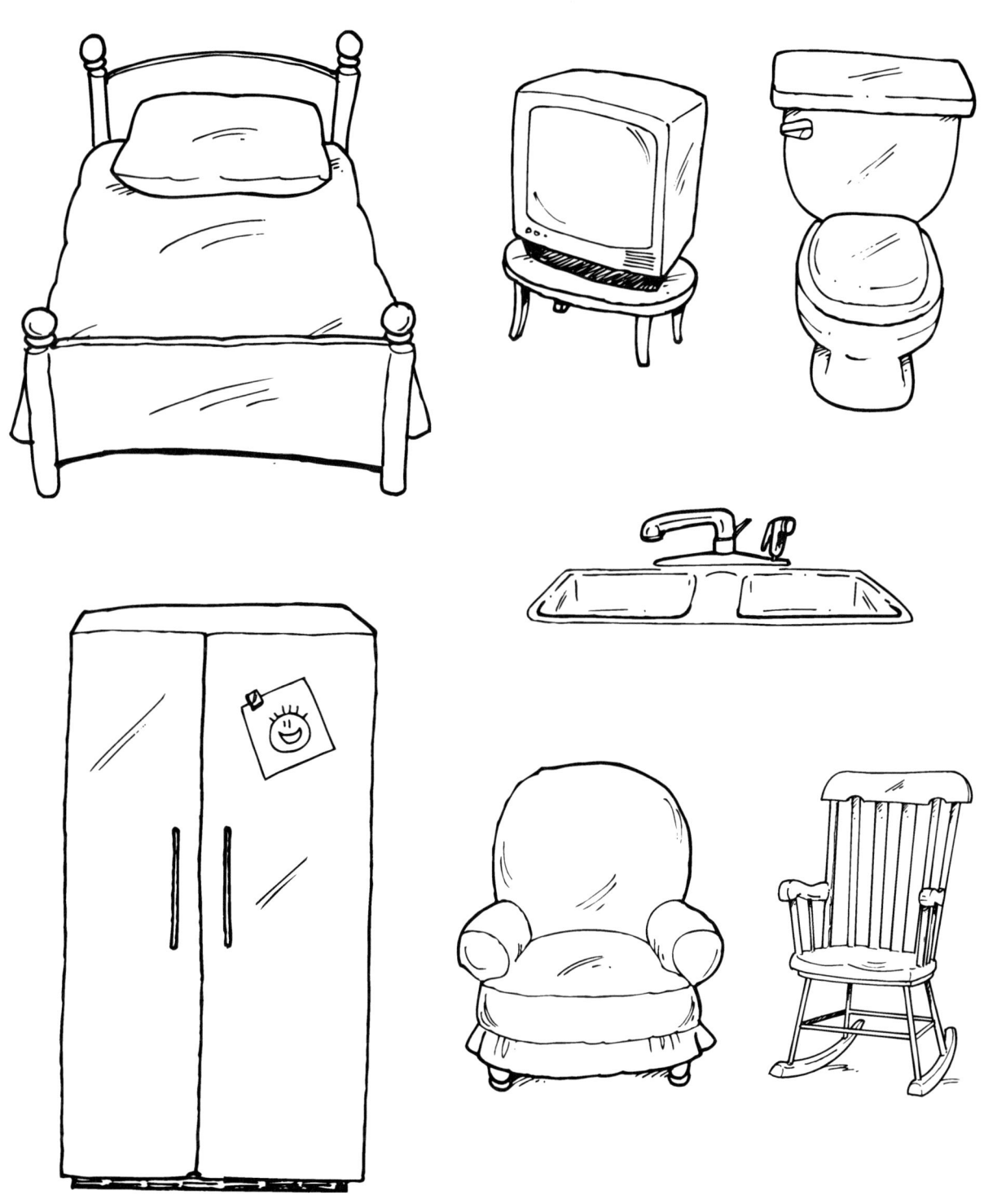

Extension Activity, continued

Cut out the household items below and on page 129. Look at the rooms on pages 131-135 and help the child decide where each picture goes. Then glue or tape it in place.

Concept Development

Extension Activity, continued

Kitchen

Extension Activity, continued

Bedroom

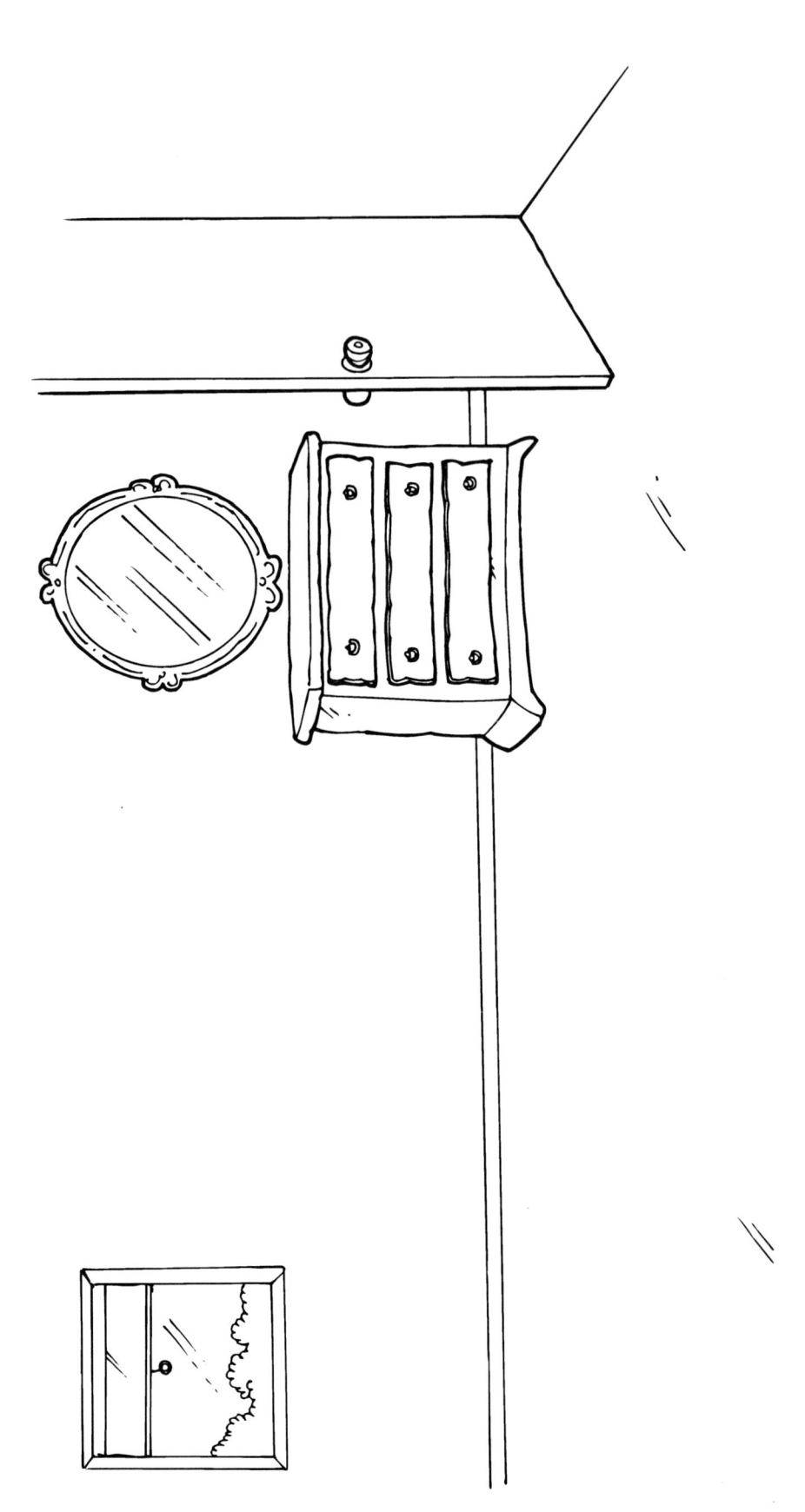

Extension Activity, continued

Bathroom

Extension Activity, continued

Living Room

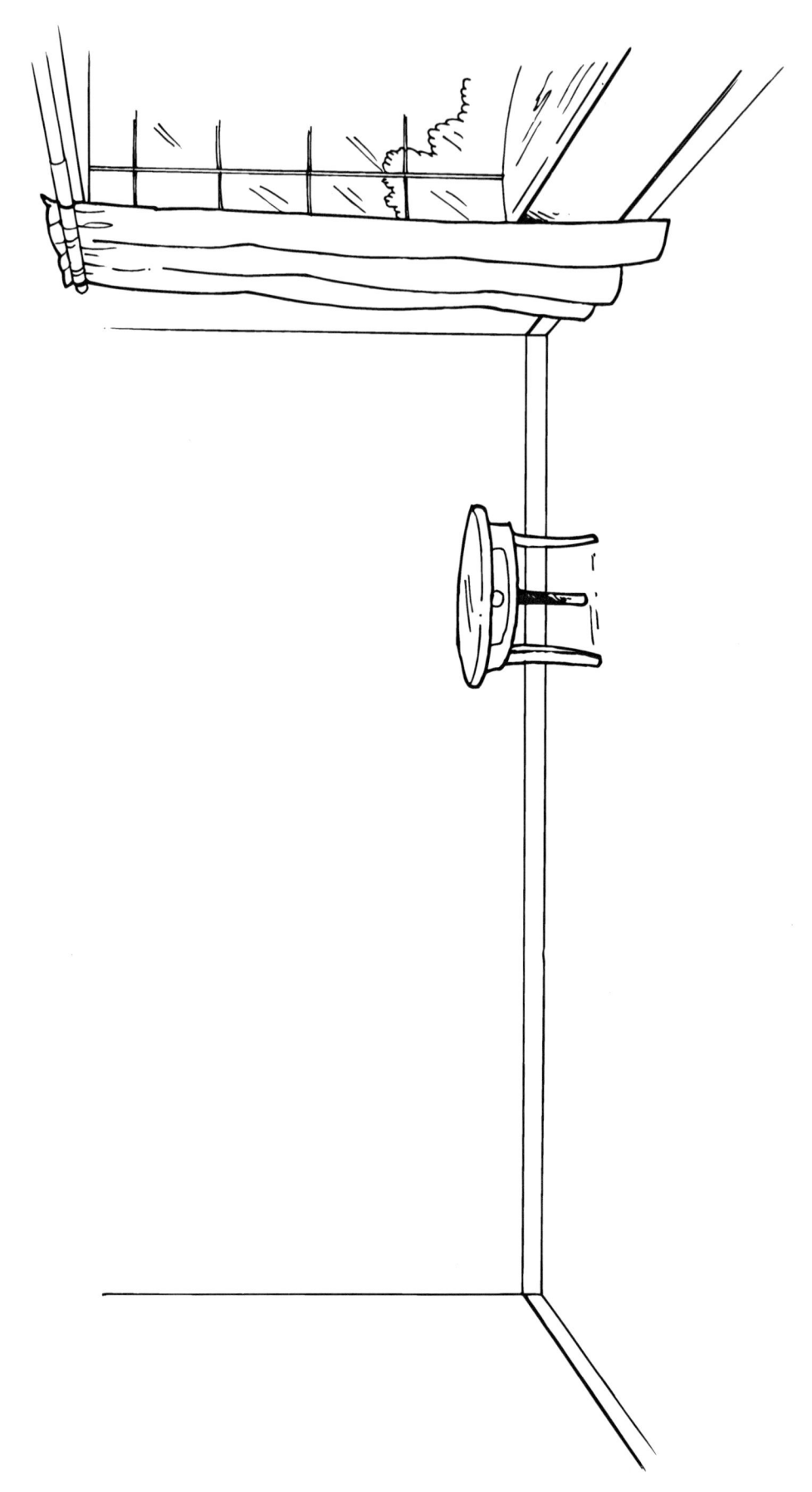

Extension Activity, continued

Dining Room

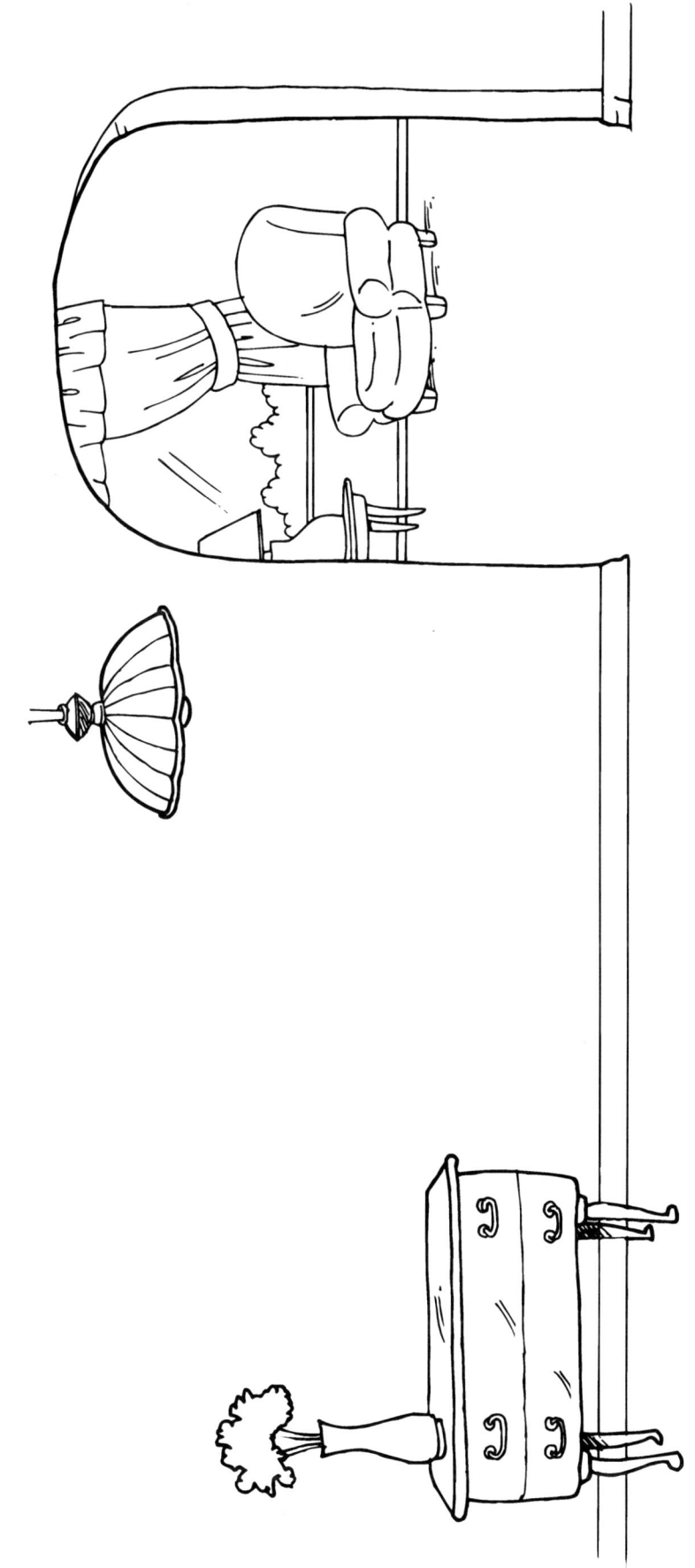

Suggested Literature

Household Items
Good Dog, Carl by Alexandra Day
Goodnight Moon by Margaret Wise Brown
Let's Look At: My Home by Nicola Tuxworth
Let's Look At: My Kitchen by Nicola Tuxworth
Maisy Goes to Bed by Lucy Cousins
Where, Oh, Where: A Sesame Street Chunky Flap Book

Chair
Chairs, Chairs, Chairs by Cynthia Cappetta

Toilet
Going to the Potty by Fred Rogers*
Toddler's Potty Book by Alida Allison

Bed
The Bed Book by Harriet Ziefert

*Text may be too difficult for some children, but the photographs are very realistic.

1-12-98